BUILD A BEAUTIFUL BUSINESS

CON CONFIANZA

Become Friends with Risk
to Grow, Scale, and Impact
(And Avoid These Mistakes!)

ROSALIE ENNES

Author photographs by Nevenka Trinajstic

For more information, email info@portecuaconsulting.cpa.

ISBN Paperback: 9798893164398
ISBN Hardcover: 9798893164206
ISBN Ebook: 9798893164381

GET YOUR FREE GIFTS!
¡UNOS REGALOS PARA TI!

Want complimentary resources that'll help you start making progress on building *your* beautiful business? I've got you covered!

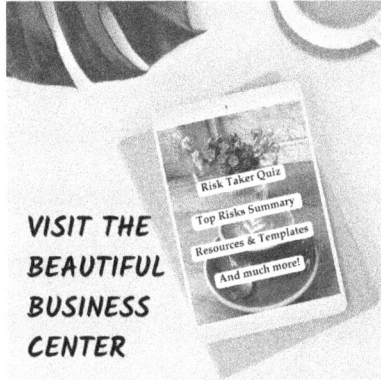

VISIT THE BEAUTIFUL BUSINESS CENTER

Risk Taker Quiz
Top Risks Summary
Resources & Templates
And much more!

For the best experience with this book, head to the Beautiful Business Center where you'll find value-packed resources, templates, and much more, including a summary of the top risks we discuss in this book, and a quiz that reveals what kind of risk taker you are.

Curated for you to implement the learnings of this book faster, this center will be your go-to place for all the latest *chisme* so you can strengthen your friendship with risk to grow, scale, and impact in the way you envision.

Scan this QR code to enter now,
or visit http://buildabeautifulbusiness.com.

Dedication

For all those who dare to build a beautiful business.

Table of Contents

PART 2 — STRATEGY

PART 3 — PROCESSES

PART 4 — TRANSFORMATION

Who This Book Is For

This book is for you if you're tired of the status quo, the less-than-stellar statistics, and the fact that women, BIPOC, and LGBTQIA+ entrepreneurs are often overlooked despite great potential—and you're ready to disrupt your way into a better future.

This book will introduce a brand-new way to view your business—with a risk lens. This new vantage point will transform how you lead your business, and will be a powerful enabler to put you in the best position to change the statistics.

And yes, I know you might want to run for the hills when you hear the word risk, but stick around. *No te vas a arrepentir.*

Told through the perspective of stories, this book will walk you through how to leverage risk to grow, scale, and impact. It'll give you the foresight as to what can go wrong and how to avoid it in your business. Along the way, you'll discover the risk frameworks, tools, and practical applications to maximize your time, money, and energy for every decision that you make and across a variety of risks you'll face as a business owner. It'll go beyond the traditional advice you've heard about how to build a business.

Across four parts—Mindset, Strategy, Processes, and Transformation—this book will take you on a journey to become friends with risk. You'll walk away feeling more confident, more protected, more resilient, and ready to build your beautiful business empowered with a risk lens.

Whether you are:

ʊ **A new, ambitious entrepreneur who loves to be prepared**

ʊ **A seasoned, innovative entrepreneur who's ready to elevate**

ʊ **Or an aspiring entrepreneur who dreams of launching their own business one day**

...this book is for you! *¿Estás lista?*

Introduction

I've come to find that many people have certain feelings about risk. Even though most will acknowledge it exists, they actively avoid thinking about it. It might seem like a scary word because you relate it to the unknown, which can be daunting. But building a business is daunting as well, and you're already doing that. It's time to become friends with risk so you can use it to your advantage.

HOW TO THINK ABOUT RISK

Risk is simply what could go wrong—challenges, pain points, weaknesses, threats, worries, fears. You've probably thought about and worked with risk already.

For instance, with a SWOT analysis (strengths, weaknesses, opportunities, and threats), you're already going through the process of identifying weaknesses and threats. And when you do a cost-benefit analysis, you're already evaluating risk even if it's not called out. Or when you complete due diligence procedures with possible new partners or investors, you're already engaging in a form of risk analysis as well.

Risk is all about the possibility of something bad happening. It doesn't mean that it actually will happen. And it doesn't mean that taking a risk is bad; it just means that to achieve something, you have to face risks that come with inherent uncertainty. Taking risks is actually a good thing, most of the time. Think about it. No risk, no reward. (You'll learn about the concept of upside risk shortly.)

For now:

Risk is something—an event, scenario, or failure—that could adversely affect the achievement of your business's objectives.

Risk management is how you go about identifying, assessing, and managing your risks.

We'll speak a lot more about risk and risk management throughout this book. *¡Qué emoción!*

WHY CARE ABOUT RISK

Your three most important resources are your time, money, and energy. Embedding a positive view toward risk will maximize all three in your business. It'll shorten the learning curve that you experience when building a business because you're proactively looking out for your business.

While making decisions, you'll anticipate consequences, assess what could go wrong, and implement actions within your business that'll strengthen it—versus waiting for sh*t to hit the fan, and then worrying about it, or spinning your wheels and getting nowhere. You'll avoid the unnecessary pain and instead, reap the benefits of using your precious resources elsewhere. It's much easier and much more cost-effective to prevent issues before they arise.

And the earlier you start, the more exponential benefits you'll get. (Just like investing, you'll have a bigger return on your investment the earlier you start.)

With a risk lens on your business, you, your leaders, and your employees will think about risk. Every decision will be made with risk in mind, which means your business will be protected and optimized even if you're not in the room because—spoiler alert!—we all manage risk. And your employees will also be used to it from early on, which is much easier than trying to teach them risk concepts later on when they're used to how things have always been done.

It's one of those things that'll pay you back many times over. Especially as an often under-resourced entrepreneur, it's essential to take advantage of anything that puts you in the best position to make your business run as well as possible. *¿Te parece bien?*

WHY THIS BOOK WAS WRITTEN

I wrote this book to empower diverse, ambitious, impact-driven entrepreneurs to build beautiful businesses—because women, BIPOC, and LGBTQIA+ entrepreneurs deserve all the same opportunities as everyone else. This book is for those who're after true impact with their business because we know it's time to do things differently. We're no longer playing small in environments that undervalue and underserve us. We're now tapping into our full potential because wealth, representation, and safe spaces should be for everyone.

And while there should be a level playing field, the reality is we don't all have the same starting line. We don't all have the generational knowledge or resources to lean on, or experiment with. We don't all get the funding we need. We don't all get approved for loans, and even when we do, they're usually in smaller amounts or with higher interest rates. Whether you're looking at the statistics of how many women-owned businesses make over six and seven figures, how much venture capital is going to BIPOC and LGBTQIA+ founders, or how many diverse founders have trouble getting financing, the statistics leave much to be desired. Whichever way you slice it, there's much more to do for an equitable entrepreneurial ecosystem.

Especially given the rapid rate at which we're starting businesses, in some cases two to eight times faster than our counterparts, leaving knowledge, resources, and funds out of our hands is a disservice to economic growth overall. We're already collectively contributing trillions in GDP, generating billions in revenue annually and directly responsible for millions of jobs. *Imagine* the potential if we did have access to everything we needed to thrive.

Despite some progress and advancements, it still feels like we have to work twice as hard to get half as far, which means we have to work four times as hard to get all the way there. Plus, we often don't get into the rooms we need to be in, and when we do, we still run the chance of being overlooked or judged for being too *this* or too *that*. Too loud, too much, too quiet, too aggressive... Not to mention the fact that when we make mistakes, they seem to be magnified. One mistake, and the outside world tells you, "I told you so."

This is why now, more than ever, we need to feel seen, heard, and empowered with the knowledge to succeed. While we can't change the existing ecosystem overnight, we can set ourselves up well if we share resources, uplift each other, and claim our seat at the table—even if it's one we build ourselves. We can cultivate a growth mindset and continue to find ways to not only survive, but demonstrate why we're here to stay. And we can move forward because we know our grit and resilience are unmatched. *Seguimos adelante como sea.*

This book is my way of providing us with a powerful lever to learn, persevere, and get ahead despite the challenges, obstacles, and scrutiny. I truly believe that with a risk lens and the knowledge, strategies, and tactics that come with it, we'll be equipped to make confident decisions that'll grow our businesses into innovative, profitable, and sustainable businesses that have long-term impact.

I want your business to give you *escalofríos* when you think about how far you've come. We're here to take up space *se ha dicho*.

WHY THE WORD BEAUTIFUL?

When deciding what word to use to define the businesses we're building, I could have used "great," "nice," "optimized," "amazing," but "beautiful" meant something special.

To me a beautiful business isn't just keeping up appearances—it's beautiful inside and out. From the product it delivers, the people who work in it, to the processes that support it, it all works together beautifully. It continuously delivers and goes beyond itself, always assessing how to make the most of any money, time, and energy put into it, in order to maximize impact on its communities.

It's also a way to redefine beauty itself. Especially in Latino culture where we've been told growing up to look pretty—hair done, makeup on, nails painted—because we never know who we're going to run into, it's a way of disrupting the traditional sense of beauty. We each define our own beauty. *¡Todas somos bellas!*

Cheers to us building a beautiful business *our* way. *¡Salud!*

WHAT TO EXPECT IN THIS BOOK

Bringing the vision of this book to life has been a journey. I knew I wanted to write this book, but what did I want to say? How did I want to convey this book to maximize impact? How could I use my career, my background, and my expertise in risk and audit to support diverse entrepreneurs and our communities? And also honor my identity and lived experiences as a woman, as a Latina, as an Ecuadorian-Portuguese American?

If you search for risk management books online, you're going to find boring, dry, technical books, and ones more aimed at risk professionals. Risk is often overlooked since it's not as sexy as topics like sales, marketing, and branding. But by embracing risk as a lens through which you make decisions for your business, you'll be able to build a successful one. That's why my aim with this book is to teach risk management concepts in an easy, conversational, and digestible way. You'll be learning without really feeling like you're learning—like a conversation between friends.

And because our communities lean so heavily on storytelling as a means to elicit emotion, teach lessons, and drive action, this book is a collection of stories. These stories, or mistakes that were made by other businesses, will show us what not to do and then together, we'll walk through the learnings and tools to prevent it in your business. I want to avoid these stories becoming yours.

Each story will be told from different perspectives too. While the stories will be mainly from the perspective of the CEO and Founder, you'll also see stories told from the perspective of various employees—because everyone can affect your business.

Through the exercises, frameworks, and reflections in this book, you'll be ready to make strong decisions, take on big goals, and handle setbacks, with ease.

This isn't to say that this book won't challenge you; it will. It actually may overwhelm you at times, *si soy sincera*. You might find you have to take a break, or that some stories don't resonate yet, and that's okay. Take your time with it. It's intentionally meant to serve you as you move through your stages (more on this in chapter 10 where I describe a business's emerging, growing, and scaling stages), so you can and should come back to it as you evolve. Each time you do, you'll be able to see things from a different viewpoint. So don't worry if the story seems unrelated to your current stage. Enjoy the *chisme* for now, and take note of the lessons *por si las necesitas en el futuro*.

This book will have a bit of Spanish as well—to pay homage *a la cultura* and the fact that Latinos are the largest demographic launching businesses. I wanted to bring my whole self to this book. (And if you don't speak Spanish, no problem. I've provided a Spanish-English dictionary at the back of this book. Think of this as a bonus opportunity to learn some Spanish!)

A quick note for the context of this book: Any time I refer to "product," I'm referring to what you sell in your business, which could be a physical product or a service. While you'll see "services" used as well, I'll primarily use "product" to mean either a product or a service.

And with that, I think we're ready to get started. *¿Empezamos?*

Your First Risk Lesson

I f I were to ask you if you're a Risk Manager, or have been one in the past, what would you say? More than likely, you're shaking your head no. (Unless you read the spoiler alert in the introduction, in which case, you're ahead of the game!)

Risk management in its traditional sense has typically been known as its own department in the business world and not introduced until much later, at which point it sits in a business in a siloed fashion. Others would even consider it to be synonymous with insurance. But it's not.

Risk management is simply the management of risks, which we all participate in.

We manage risks every day, even in our personal lives. When we look both ways before crossing the street, we're making a risk decision. If we cross even though a car is coming, we have likely assessed that we have enough time to cross, *antes de que nos aplasten como una cucaracha jaja*. The same goes for whether we drive the speed limit, buy home insurance, adopt a dog, get on a plane, or let our phone store our passwords. We make risk decisions daily even if we don't realize it.

Even deciding to open your business is a risk decision, so from day one you're managing risk. After that, you're deciding whether or not to launch a product, offer a new service, sign a contract, protect your customer data, bring on a partner, implement a system...you get the idea. We'll cover these and many more scenarios throughout this book.

So, do you manage risk?

Hopefully you're now nodding your head yes, instead of no.

MAKING RISK DECISIONS IN YOUR BUSINESS

You might be now asking yourself, "What risk decisions have I made in my business?"

In some of the decisions you made, you likely went through your process of weighing the pros and cons, or researching possibilities or alternatives, and *then* you made a decision. An action was taken.

At its core, there are four actions you take when managing risk in your business. You can accept, avoid, mitigate, or transfer risk (**AAMT**).

- **Accept** is what it sounds like. You went through your process, and decided to move forward with your plan and accept existing circumstances.

- **Avoid** is also what it sounds like. You instead decided to let go of your plan, and focused your attention elsewhere.

- **Mitigate** is what usually happens. You decided to move forward with your plan, but not before putting something in place to prevent or reduce the likelihood of a bad outcome.

- **Transfer** is what happens when you put it in someone else's hands. You decided to move forward with your plan, but wanted to give the potential consequences to someone else.

Here are three quick examples so you see these actions *in action*.

In your personal life, you keep your dog on a leash to ____ the risk of them running away. The answer would be <u>avoid</u>. (Unless your dog is superstrong, in which case the answer might be <u>mitigate</u>.)

In your business, you sign a contract with a vendor to ____ the risk of misunderstandings. Here you're using a contract as a way to <u>mitigate</u> the risk of misunderstandings.

Okay, now a fun one because, I promise, risk is fun. *¡Te lo prometo!*

You arrive at an event and are about to enter through the door, but you have so many things in your hand—your wallet, laptop bag, iced coffee, keys, etc. You don't want to drop everything, so you have to decide how to open the door. In this scenario, you have all actions available to you and what you decide to do will depend on your preference.

If you accept the risk, you walk through with everything. If you avoid the risk, you wait for someone to open the door for you. If you mitigate the risk, you ask someone else to hold your wallet and keys. If you transfer the risk, you give all your stuff to someone else.

See? Not so bad, right?

The great thing about risk management is that you decide how you want to manage it. Your approach is unique to your business and your risk appetite.

THE TYPES OF RISK

And now you might be asking yourself, "What types of risk should I watch out for in my business?"

Well, the short answer is there are hundreds. Risks are everywhere and they have layers. But at the highest level, there are five types of risks you want to think about as you build your beautiful business that conveniently have an acronym of **SOFTR**. Let's think of them as soft risks because risks aren't so bad. (Although maybe you don't believe me yet, but you will by the end of this book.)

There are five categories all risks fit into:

- **Strategic risks** are those that could affect your business and prevent it from achieving its goals and objectives (e.g., planning, product, sales and marketing, business development, culture, reputation).

- **Operational risks** are those that could affect your daily business activities and cause internal inefficiencies, failures, or frauds to occur (e.g., sourcing, fulfillment, inventory management, accounts payable, payroll).

- **Financial risks** are those that could affect your ability to maintain integrity in your numbers and put you in a position to report out on numbers that are inaccurate, incomplete, or untimely (e.g., financial reporting, account reconciliations, accounting treatment, revenue recognition, taxes).

- **Technology risks**, also known as IT and cybersecurity risks, are those that create the potential for a system failure or breach to disrupt your business (e.g., unauthorized access, interface errors, cyberattacks, phishing, service outages).

- **Regulatory risks**, also known as compliance risks, are those that have to do with how well your business can abide by legal or regulatory requirements (i.e., SOX, PCI, data privacy, HIPAA).

If this all seems like gibberish, remember it's okay, and it's okay to let yourself be overwhelmed by risk for now.

Everything will make much more sense as you become friends with risk through this book.

WHAT'S NEXT

You might have wanted to run far, far away when I started talking about risk, *pero no te me escondas*. I'm glad you're here and still with me. Let's build your beautiful business.

Up next, we'll begin with part 1: Mindset.

Part 1

MINDSET

Chapter 1

Manage Your Mindset with Confidence: Letting Doubts and Pressures Take Over Will Stop You from Taking Action

Starting and running a business isn't easy. It's not uncommon to find yourself filled with thoughts about your abilities. "Can I do it?" "Am I doing it right?" "Is this what I should do?" You might question yourself every step of the way, and you may even push yourself more than is healthy at times. In this chapter, we'll talk about how you can leverage a risk mindset to confidently take action as you build your beautiful business.

I think I can do it, but can I?
POV: CEO and Founder

I had ideas. Big ones.

It never felt like they were heard though. While I tried to contribute, the conversations always seemed to center around how things were traditionally done. I often found myself looking around the conference room, seeing no representation and feeling like the "only." I was frustrated every day.

One day it was because I couldn't get a word in.

Another day it was because I was interrupted.

Another day it was because my idea was dismissed.

The truth was my perspective was different from my colleagues. My life experiences and cultural upbringing made it so that I couldn't see things from their exact vantage point. And while I attempted to understand theirs, they didn't try to understand mine. Not really.

That day we were sitting around the table talking about launching a new product. It was clear they had one buyer in mind and wanted to keep things status quo. They shot down my ideas as usual.

I had enough.

There was no way I wanted to be in that space anymore. There was something missing. I wanted to create a new space that shifted the way things were done, and allowed for change to happen. I wanted to meet the unmet needs of the overlooked buyers. I wanted to be valued for my contributions and to create value for others. I realized I had a bigger purpose.

But, was it possible for me to do it? Could I learn everything I need to know? Could I run a business? **I think I can do it, but can I?**

~

YOU WERE MEANT TO DISRUPT

Whether it was a natural pull, a gentle push, or a specific moment that you said, "I've had it," entrepreneurship has called you in. Welcome.

You're here because you want to disrupt the existing landscape. You want to change the way things are done. You want to take your shot at running your own business because you have so much to offer. Between your life experiences, cultural upbringing, and maybe even some "what not to do" lessons from corporate roles, all of it will serve you in this new chapter. All of it will help shape how you build, run, and lead your business.

And while you know you have the passion and drive toward a better future, it doesn't mean doubts won't creep in. It doesn't mean you won't find yourself doubting if you can do it, or maybe even doubting your worth at times. But you know your worth, and now it's time to scale your worth. This is how you'll have exponential impact.

For all this to work, you have to be confident that entrepreneurship is your path and that you're ready to overcome any doubts like a pro. You can't let doubts stop you from pursuing your idea, vision, or dream.

OUR FIRST RISK ASSESSMENT TOGETHER

Risk assessment. What's that?

Simply, it's the process you go through to assess if an action is worth taking. It's how you make decisions.

Technically, a **risk assessment** is performed when you evaluate the likelihood (probability) and impact (consequence) of an event, scenario, or failure occurring for you.

To determine if entrepreneurship is the right path, I always recommend starting out with a "Start a Business" risk assessment that has three critical elements to it. For those who have already taken the plunge, consider this your recommitment to it.

- **Product** – Is the product you want to deliver needed? Does it have an audience? Is there an unmet need for it? This doesn't mean it necessarily has to exist in its current form, but it does mean you should make sure you've talked to enough people to know if there's demand for it. (Or that you have enough belief in your vision that it'll have value once you educate people about it.)

- **Finances** – Where will you get the money to start your business? Savings, loans, credit cards, investors? Do you know how much the first year will cost you? Do you know much you'll make in your first year? Or how much time it'll take to turn a profit? I highly recommend you create a high-level budget to give you peace of mind. Every *centavito* matters, especially in the first year.

- **Timing** – Is it the appropriate time to launch? Are you ready to take on this type of commitment mentally, physically, and emotionally? Are you going to take it on full force, or are you going to take it on alongside your nine-to-five? In an era where many employees are starting side hustles, this is a great way to ease into it if that's where your comfort level is.

Congratulations, you've done your first risk assessment! You're prepared to move forward with entrepreneurship.

DOUBTS ARE JUST THOUGHTS

Now that you know you want to do it, know that you *can* do it. *¡Sí, se puede!*

Any doubts that come up are just thoughts. There's so much you can do. And you know it too. Your ancestors didn't make sacrifices and endure hardship for you to doubt yourself.

That being said, having some doubts is normal. Every entrepreneur has them no matter the stage—as you start, as you hire, as you launch, as you pitch. For many of us, it's the first time we're doing this thing called entrepreneurship. Some days it might feel like you have everything together, and other days it might feel like everything is falling apart. Some days might feel like both. (You might even be tempted to leave it all behind some days.)

The important thing is to know how to handle those moments or days of doubts. We're only human after all. Allow yourself to process it, feel what comes up, then flow through it. You don't want to let the doubts slow you down or stop you from taking action. You don't want the doubts to change your mind about going to that networking event, launching that program, or putting yourself into all the spaces your business belongs.

And you especially don't want to let doubts cause you to tell yourself "no" without even trying (e.g., not applying to a grant or following up with a potential client). I know it's happened to some of us. Let others tell you no; don't do it for them.

LET'S TALK ABOUT UPSIDE RISK

Whether you knew it or not, from the time you took the plunge into entrepreneurship, and every time you've overcome doubts since then, you've interacted with risk. Upside risk, specifically.

Upside risk is the required risk you need to take on to achieve your vision. In it lies all the amazing potential and limitless possibilities for your business. You need it in order to grow and scale. Think new product line, market expansion, system implementation, for example. All these initiatives will bring up doubts as you're embarking on them, but you forge ahead because you know it'll be positive for your business and its impact. *Sí, por favor.*

(Downside risk is likely what you're used to hearing about when you think about risk. And it might scare you. These are the risks you want to stay away from, and avoid at all costs. Think safety incidents, lawsuits, hackers, for instance. *No, gracias.* We'll take on all the upside risk please.)

MOVE FORWARD WITH CONFIDENCE

Don't dim your light because you're afraid or cautious of what could happen. Believe in yourself and your abilities. You can build a beautiful business *con confianza!*

Take a few moments to reflect on your entrepreneurship adventure so far, and any doubts you've had during it. When was the last time you doubted yourself? Did you flow through it or did you let the doubts stop you from taking action? Are there some recurring doubts that stop you from putting your business out there? How can you make sure you move forward with confidence next time?

I question myself, more than I care to admit.
POV: CEO and Founder

When the opportunity first presented itself, I said, "Why not?"

But now that I was about to be in the room pitching my business for its biggest investment so far, I was nervous, sweaty, and feeling like I would rather be anywhere else but here. I had been preparing for weeks, but now it all came down to this presentation.

From the outside, my team thought I exuded confidence.

I can't say it's not true. From the outside, I appeared confident. The media loved me. I was featured in articles. I was on a new podcast every month. I was spotlighted for Hispanic Heritage Month every year. I was constantly recognized for top-tier branding and marketing.

But behind the scenes, I wasn't as confident. I was worried about our cash flow. I was worried about making payroll. I didn't know if our new launch was going to do well. I didn't know if I would be a good manager now that we were expanding our team. I wasn't sure if any of the decisions I was making were the right ones.

And now with the presentation looming, I had no idea if the investors would see our potential.

So many questions today, and every day.

I question myself, more than I care to admit.

~

NOT FOR THE FAINT OF HEART

I won't lie—and you probably already know this depending on where you are in your entrepreneurial journey—starting a business is just the first step.

Building a business, a beautiful one, isn't for the faint of heart. It'll require intention, execution, and tears. *Vas a llorar. Veremos si de emoción o de tristeza. Probablemente de los dos.*

Just like we talked about how it's normal to have doubts as to whether you can do it (and you can!), questioning all your decisions throughout is also part of the process. Every time we do things outside of our comfort zone, we stretch ourselves to do what we've never done before and may not feel comfortable doing. Silver lining: it means we're expanding our capacity.

THERE'S ALWAYS SOMETHING TO LEARN

We're continuously learning how to run a business and how to be a leader. That never stops whether you're a new entrepreneur or a seasoned one.

Because when you learn one thing, there'll be something else to learn. When you make a decision, there'll be another one to make. When you solve one problem, there'll be more. The decisions will get bigger. The problems will get bigger. The decisions and problems multiply as you grow and scale your business.

So you need to get better. This is why it's so important that as a leader, you never stop learning. The good news is that if you're questioning your decisions, it means you're on the right path. And the great news is that it means you already are adopting a risk mindset when it comes to building your business.

IT'S TIME FOR AN IMPOSTER SYNDROME REFRAME

Repito. It's normal to question yourself. It's normal to feel what you've known for so long as imposter syndrome.

But move over, imposter syndrome. *Fuera de aquí.* It's time for a reframe.

Imposter syndrome is really your risk mindset talking to you. It's your mind's way of signaling you to possible risks. It's giving you the opportunity to react, and take control of next steps. And there are many ways to react depending on what that signal is. The key is to recognize what it means in order to handle it effectively.

Here are some examples of what it could mean.

Is it a momentary lapse of confidence? Give yourself a pep talk. Bring it! Sometimes we need that. You prepared for this. You worked hard for this. You got this. If you have a personal *f**k yeah!* moments list going, this is a great time to review all your wins. (If you don't, start one today!) And if all else fails, fake it until you make it. This isn't about being inauthentic, it's about pushing yourself to the next version that might seem "fake" to the current version of yourself. This version is real and is coming.

Is it a lack of knowledge? Maybe you're doing something for the first time, and you don't feel like you know enough to feel ready. Do more research. Seek out expertise in the area you're learning in. Find those that are eager to share what they know, and how they approached learning what was once unfamiliar to them. Find the non-gatekeepers, and be a sponge. *De donde come uno comen dos.*

Is it a need for guidance? We're community driven, so don't isolate yourself as you build your business. Don't do it alone. That's what we're here for. Find the memberships, communities, masterminds, books, podcasts that you need to guide you, help you, and push you. Find your business BFFs that you can lean on, and vent to, in the good times and bad. *¡Juntas somos más fuertes!*

Is it a thought that diverse entrepreneurs struggle with? As we talk more and more about our stories, about privilege, we realize how much our immediate environment, societal expectations, or systems put in place may have not been built for us. Knowing this doesn't mean you can't achieve your dreams. Filter through these thoughts, and find ways to set them down if they don't serve you. If anything, use this to connect with others who can relate to make your impact stronger (more about this later on in this book).

DON'T LET OTHERS' THOUGHTS
SEEP INTO YOUR THOUGHTS

And sometimes we question ourselves because others have questioned us, and it seeped into our thoughts.

Early in my career, I had a boss tell me I shouldn't consider doing an international rotation to Latin America because women weren't respected there. Could this have easily deterred me from even thinking about working in Latin America in the future? Absolutely. Did it? No. Fast forward a year, and I was traveling to manage and lead risk-based audits in Mexico, Chile, and Brazil, conducting meetings and presenting findings in Spanish and Portuguese, and was being requested to go do a risk and controls assessment for a new system implementation. I didn't let their thoughts influence me.

Recognize when thoughts are valid. *Y fuera con tonterías.*

Don't stunt your growth and impact because you question yourself so much that you let it affect you. We all question ourselves. We're all learning. We don't know everything and we never will.

REFRAME IT NEXT TIME

The next time you question your decisions or feel a bit of imposter syndrome rearing its head, reframe it. Thank your risk mindset for the questions. And let it guide you toward the next step. Like the song says, "*¡No pare, sigue, sigue! ¡No pare, sigue, sigue!*"

I put so much pressure on myself and toppled, literally.

POV: CEO and Founder

When we won the bid against other more established businesses, we were ecstatic.

It was one of the largest projects we'd had so far so we had a lot riding on it. From the beginning, we hit the ground running. We held planning meetings. We set up a timeline, and communicated it with our project team and to the client. The deadline was clear, and we knew time would fly, so we went full speed ahead to ensure successful delivery of this project.

As the team prepared the deliverables one by one, our days started getting longer. We knew some days may require longer hours. I knew personally I would be working more and more. But what happened in the last month I didn't anticipate. All the work came to me for review, and re-review, as they submitted the updated files. We also had other projects happening at the same time, which started taking a toll on me. I had to get it done though. I started working evenings and eating dinner with my computer.

There was an intense energy that I could feel building up inside of me. I knew I was close to burnout, but I just kept telling myself I should push myself now and the break would come later.

We came to the last week of the project, and it was Tuesday morning, the day of our weekly team meeting. I went to the break room to grab some water before we started. On my way back, I was thinking about everything I had to talk to the team about. I was thinking about what the next few days would look like. I knew sleep would be nonexistent.

Thinking about sleep, I felt myself falling. Sure enough, I was falling against the wall.

A colleague came to help me up. Reality hit. I had fainted against the wall. **I put so much pressure on myself and toppled, literally.**

~

ENTREPRENEURSHIP WILL TEST YOUR LIMITS

Entrepreneurship will challenge you, in ways you imagine—and in ways you never imagined. There'll be many moments that'll take your breath away.

Whether it's a big project, a large catering gig, or a massive wholesale order, we want to do it well. We want to meet deadlines, and in many cases, rise to the occasion because building a business has us doing things we haven't done before.

And because we have such a strong work ethic and don't want to let ourselves or others down, we push ourselves. It's why people continue to work after fainting in the office, take client calls in the hospital after a major surgery, and work through being sick. So much is riding on our shoulders to succeed. We put an extraordinary amount of pressure on ourselves to perform, and to be perfect, it's a wonder we don't topple more.

Plus, we know that what we do is incredibly scrutinized. If we don't meet deadlines, if we go over budget, if we move meetings, if we're nervous during our presentation, if our sales aren't where they should be, these missteps are magnified. "Oh, they did *xyz*—we shouldn't have given them a chance. No wonder." While others can fail, we can't. *¿Hablo verdades o no?*

TAKE CARE OF YOUR BIGGEST ASSET: YOU

You started your businesses because you wanted to make a difference. You wanted to do the right thing, and build it the right way.

But you're the biggest asset in your business, so take care of yourself.

Because there's always something new. Every time we cross things off the to-do list, more things get added on. Every time we think we're at the goal line, the goal post moves. It's equally important to master the art of saying yes as it is to master the art of saying no. It's a muscle that you'll continuously learn to flex.

Building a beautiful business takes time and effort. The likelihood of your first years in business being a breeze is unlikely. And we don't want to do it at the cost of our well-being. It's important to define what entrepreneur self-care looks like for you.

PAY ATTENTION TO THE SIGNS

We can rise to many occasions, *porque somos magníficas*, and we're resilient to the max, but we have to know when it's time to pay attention to the signs. We have to let our risk mindset guide us to what needs to change.

And this isn't to say there won't be hard days. It's unavoidable. Deadlines happen. Big projects need to get done. Orders need to get fulfilled. You'll experience periods where you're overwhelmed. But if you find yourself constantly saying, "Tomorrow will be better," Houston, *tenemos un problema*.

The risk here is that you ignore the signs, leading you to overwhelm, burnout, and health consequences that take you out—literally.

Remember: we're no longer in survival mode and we no longer have to let perfectionism dictate our lives. We don't have to have it all figured out. We can ask for help. We can lean on the community, and we should. We can delegate. We can push that meeting. We can reprioritize. We can adjust deliverables (some of them really are "done is better than perfect.") We can say no to things.

DON'T LET YOUR TANK RUN EMPTY

And don't forget that you set an example for your team. You set the tone at the top for what really matters, and what's acceptable. Do you want to show them that working when you shouldn't is okay? Is it okay to accept the potential of burnout and health risks?

Become friends with risk by identifying how close you are to an empty tank, and doing something about it, before it manifests itself into something you can't control—and something that affects your team. This is known as risk identification and risk response (or mitigation)—more on this later.

And give yourself some grace *por favor.* We're doing hard things.

WHAT'S YOUR RISK OF TOPPLING?

So, how close are you to toppling? Let's do a burnout risk assessment.

If you've been saying, "I'll get a break soon," but the break never comes, and it's been over thirty days, you're dangerously close to toppling. Do something ASAP. Something isn't working in your business. Figure out what you should prioritize and what you can move, adjust, or remove for the next six months.

If you've been saying, "I've been burning the midnight oil most days, but I disconnect on the weekends," you're staying afloat, but there are danger flags in the distance. Spend some time looking at your priorities for the next three months and readjust so that you have a larger time period to recharge and reset.

If you've been saying, "I'm working hard, but I take breaks, and there's a longer break in sight. *Me largo de aquí y me voy de vacaciones,*" then you're doing it right. Instead, phone an entrepreneur friend and ask them how close they are to toppling, and help them out.

Chapter 2

Make Informed Decisions: Without Proper Analysis, Your Mind Will Run Wild and Keep You Up at Night

As a business owner, there are a million thoughts that run through your head 24/7, many of which probably keep you up at night. Whether you're worried about securing funding, sustaining revenue growth, or expanding successfully into new channels, there'll always be something that's weighing heavily on your mind. In this chapter, we'll address how you can use a risk mindset to work through important decisions in your business so your mind can rest more peacefully during the day, and into the night.

My funding might not come.
POV: CEO and Founder

I don't know how people do it.

I was pitching left and right, talking to anyone and everyone who would talk to me about my business. I knew I needed the funding. And I knew I needed business partners who would support and advise me on how to build my business. So even when I didn't want to, and every fiber in my body was telling me to rest, or do absolutely anything else, I kept sending the emails. I kept making the calls. I kept pitching my business.

Some conversations were a "no" off the bat. I struggled with those at first, but after a while, they became normal. I think I became numb to them, and kept it moving. Especially knowing that so few women founders receive funding, I knew those no's would come, but that didn't stop it from stinging. It didn't stop me from persisting because I believed in my vision.

We had a few interested investors that went into the conversation stage, but we quickly realized some of them just wanted to meet a quota to be able to say that they did consider diverse founders. Their tone told it all. Others thought it was fair game to comment on our appearance, and make passes at us during the presentation.

*At one point, we felt really good about one investor in particular. We had several conversations with them and things seemed promising. Until they decided it was appropriate to ask me out. I said no, and of course, the funding conversations stopped. It was so deflating. **My funding might not come.***

~

FIRST THINGS FIRST

Investors need to do better. Women have enough challenges. They shouldn't be sought after under false pretenses, or dismissed because they didn't accept your invite. Women are here to build beautiful businesses. *¡Déjalas, por favor!*

NOTHING ABOUT GETTING FUNDING IS EASY

Obtaining funding is a grueling process. We generally aren't the types of founders that have friends or family to lend us thousands of dollars, or close ties to wealthy investors that can easily access thousands, or millions, for you to *test out* your idea.

Whether you're pursuing funding in the form of investments, loans, or grants, all of it is exhausting. You put yourself out there, and get so many rejections. You wonder why you spent all those hours putting together that pitch or application when it could have been spent on reaching out to potential customers, making products, or posting content.

With so many rejections, you may start to question why you started your business. You may start to question if you're doing something that's worth it.

Hopefully, you come back to your why, and get grounded again.

GO FOR NO, AND EVENTUALLY YOU'LL GET A YES

Yes, there will be no's. But the no's will make the yeses so much sweeter.

Granted, it might not be exactly as you envisioned. Maybe instead of seeking investment, you decide to put more effort into submitting paperwork for loans, or applying for grants. Or maybe you decide to use credit cards to get you by at first. (They usually don't say no, but they'll drain you with high interest rates, so be sure to leverage 0% introductory rates for as long as possible. It's not a long-term solution, but it'll help you pay for investments initially while you start to generate revenue from your business.)

Educate yourself on all types of funding and lean on others. Ask for advice. Ask for intros. Plant seeds and build those relationships. Don't risk not getting the funding you need!

DON'T ACCEPT CASH FROM JUST ANYONE

Always take the time to find the right funding partners that work for you and your business. A cash injection isn't worth it if it's going to bring other consequences.

Especially when you're seeking investors, you're giving up control, and you'll have responsibilities and expectations placed upon you. You might find yourself having wanted to own your business, but now it just feels like you have a new boss, or bosses. (There's something to be said about bootstrapping for as long as possible. You can build your brand, launch products, and make financial decisions based on what works for you, versus having other opinions early on. If you can, make it work without investors.)

SURROUND YOURSELF WITH THE RIGHT PEOPLE

We're talking about funding here, but the same goes for any type of partnership that you engage in as you build your business—collaborations with other businesses, influencers, ambassadors, vendors, retailers, even acquisitions. Who you surround yourself with can make or break your success. The third parties you work with matter. *Dime con quién andas y te diré quién eres.*

You, and your team, should be clear on who you seek to partner with. Your values. Your work ethic. Your views on social issues, reproductive rights, international conflicts, all of it. Of course, it's impossible to agree on everything, but you have to know what you're aiming for. Know what your nonnegotiables are.

This will also help make it clear what your risk appetite is.

Risk appetite is the level of risk that you're willing to accept in pursuit of your business goals. It's the bar that you set for how you run your business, for yourself and your employees. For instance, with partnerships, maybe you only care about being aligned on one specific issue. Or maybe you want someone who mostly has the same views as you. Or maybe you want everyone you work with to have exactly the same views. Every business will determine its own risk appetite when it comes to a specific topic.

From there, you'll want to understand how far you're willing to move away from this bar.

Risk tolerance is the amount of deviation from your risk appetite you're willing to accept with your actions. Maybe you want no deviation, meaning that once your risk appetite is set, your risk tolerance is zero. Or maybe you're okay with some deviation. Or maybe you don't mind a large deviation. Generally, I wouldn't recommend a large deviation, unless you have a high pain threshold!

HOLD OUT FOR THE RIGHT PARTNERS

The risk here is that you aren't able to choose the right partnerships in your business that'll help you build and achieve your vision, and instead, you choose ones that could stall or hinder your brand. This all falls into reputational risk, which we'll talk much more about throughout this book.

You always want to make decisions that protect your reputation. We're building to impact here, so let's make sure we create ecosystems we're proud of.

I've seen businesses question why they pursued certain investors. I've seen businesses regret who they chose as an ambassador. I've seen businesses lose out on sales because of who they funded politically. I've seen acquisitions flop because, while it looked great on paper, the businesses were too different. How they made decisions, how they spent money, how the leaders managed the business. It can come from different angles, so be careful who you partner with. *Mejor sola que mal acompañada.*

CALL YOUR ENTREPRENEUR FRIENDS

Become friends with risk by doing sufficient research, doing your due diligence, making expectations clear, and listening to your intuition when it comes to partnerships.

In your next conversation with your entrepreneur friends, ask them which partnerships they engaged in that they wish they hadn't, or what questions they should have known to ask. *¡Que te cuenten el chisme!*

BONUS: TAKE A DEEPER DIVE

If you're finding yourself at that uncomfortable point where you've reached out to hundreds of investors and sought out what seems like all options, figure out the pivot. It might be a pivot in your business model. Maybe you pause part of your offerings to slow the burn and free up time to focus on one offering. Maybe you consider selling part of your business to bring in some capital. It might be a pivot to a new business. Maybe you have another idea or skill set that you could monetize.

Especially for us, many of us have side businesses to fund our main business. We work with what we got, right? Our resilience is like no other. It might even be that you have to take on a nine-to-five again for three, six, or twelve months. I know—not ideal. But it's not a sign of failure—it's a sign of strength, grit, and tenacity fueled by our passion for our business. If the funding isn't coming from others, we can create it ourselves.

Will this revenue bubble burst?
POV: CEO and Founder

Everyone loved our product.

I knew some would, but the fact that we kept selling out was amazing. It didn't matter the color, the style, or the length—press-on nails seemed to be what everyone wanted. It didn't even seem to matter what we priced them at. They flew off the shelves. Whereas the press-on nails of the past never stayed on well, we had developed a quality adhesive that kept them on. That combined with our bright colors and fun designs made them irresistible for our customers. Not to mention that our marketing and PR features gave us enough buzz to keep us selling rapidly.

We grew and grew, so we hired a team to help us manage our orders. We were at full capacity most days and we kept selling out faster than we could really keep up with.

At the rate we were going, sales were on an upward trend for the foreseeable future. If the next couple years were anything like the past couple years, we were looking at doubling every year. The future looked bright. We started making big plans for where we could take our business, expanding beyond direct to consumer (DTC), growing our team, and finally transitioning out of our home setup.

For our next order, we wanted to get ahead of demand and order more inventory. We wanted to stop selling out so fast, and have inventory on hand. We also wanted to increase our assortment of both colors and designs to keep our customers happy. We told our customers to hang tight because big things were coming. We put all the wheels in motion.

What we didn't expect was a new trend in nails.

Slowly we saw articles coming out about natural nails. It was all about being real, raw, and authentic. I had no doubt that press-on nails would always have a place in the market, but would it be much less than anticipated?

A wave of worry washed over me. **Will this revenue bubble burst?**

~

TRENDS COME AND GO, AND COME BACK (SOMETIMES)

Trends, am I right? We've seen trends come and go over our lifetime. Many of us have now lived long enough to see trends come back. *¡Nos estamos poniendo viejitas—jaja!* Black choker necklaces, shoulder bags, low-rise jeans, ringtones, fidget spinners, to name a few. *¿Te acuerdas?*

It's no doubt that when you have a product that takes off, it's an amazing feeling. You feel like you've unlocked something great. You have product-market fit. People love it. People keep buying. However, especially in the beginning of your business or as you launch something new, it's so important to be aware of how much your product is based on trends. And more importantly, where that trend is going. This way you follow along its journey so as to not put your business in danger, or get stuck with inventory no one wants.

IS YOUR PRODUCT SENSITIVE TO TRENDS?

Your mind might go to obvious big trends where you know the bubble will burst at some point, but taking it a step further, this is about how sensitive your product is to its ecosystem. This includes trends in personalities, behaviors, and perspectives on current events whether economic, political, or social. The risk here is that you overlook the effect of trends on sales growth, leading you to incorrectly assume continuous hyper growth year-over-year (YoY).

On a micro level, this might look like slang terms that you put on a sweatshirt but within a few months, there's new slang and you're left with a 500-sweatshirt run that no one will buy. On a macro level, this might look like a major catastrophic event that drives more people to stay home and therefore buy more at-home items and online services, but once that shifts, consumer behavior reverts back to buying outdoor items, going on vacations, and attending in-person events.

Your product may be based solely on trends, may incorporate trends, or may have very little to do with trends. You want to know where you fall on the spectrum. Find your place in the market, assess your sensitivity, and continuously monitor it. This way you'll be better prepared when it comes to changes in the market.

OTHER WAYS TO BURST YOUR REVENUE BUBBLE

And just like you don't want the revenue bubble to burst because of a trend, you also don't want it to burst because you've added too much too soon. I'm talking here about the number of revenue streams and the number of products you launch in your business.

It's likely you have so many ideas when it comes to what products you want to sell and where you want to sell them. But just because an idea is there doesn't mean you have to execute on it. You might even have customers asking, begging, for a new style or a whole new product or service. *Can you make this in green? Can you make this round? Can we customize the font? Can you make nail polish too? Can you make a course for this?* But exercise caution. *Ten cuidado.* Just because a customer wants it doesn't mean you have to do it. Just because the opportunity is there doesn't mean you have to say yes. And the more capital-intensive of a business you have, think consulting vs. candles, the more you should prioritize making the right decision that makes sense for *your* business.

Before the next few paragraphs make you feel a certain way—yes, I know many of us are multi-passionate, me included. I'm not advocating for you to limit yourself, but for you to be intentional with how you release all your wonderful ideas. *How* you add new revenue streams and add new products matters because the ultimate goal is long-lasting impact.

THE THREE S'S TO KEEP IN MIND

An easy way to assess your business is with the three S's: sensitivity, simplicity, and saturation. We've already talked about sensitivity, so let's get into simplicity next.

The simpler you can keep things, especially in the first few years will help you build a strong foundation for your brand, for your operations, and for your customer. You're finding your way in the online space or getting to know your retailers. You're figuring out how your customer thinks, buys, and why they purchase your product. And you're designing marketing, processes, and systems around that.

Each new revenue stream, and color or style you introduce, however straightforward it might seem, introduces a new layer of complexity to your business and potentially additional costs. You don't want to risk overcomplicating and stretching your small, but mighty team in so many directions. Simplify to strengthen what you have first. Introduce new streams and new products over time. You want your customer to buy from you for the long term, instead of going on a spending spree initially and disappearing, or instead of being overwhelmed with too many options. Keep it simple for them too.

As for saturation, go deep before you spread out. Every time you add a new revenue stream or new product, you're in a way creating a new business. Even if there are synergies between revenue streams, you'll need to treat each one differently. Your customer might have a whole new profile. Your stakeholders might be different. Your materials might be different. Your suppliers might be different. Your processes will be different, again stretching your team even further.

If the market is big enough, you should stay where you are as long as possible before introducing a brand-new revenue stream or product. Revenue will still increase because you have time to focus and gain more customers.

If you're trying to grow and scale your business into a one with staying power, think sensitivity, simplicity, and saturation — the three S's!

I don't want your revenue bubble to burst. In fact, I want it to be as strong as possible. *Cuanto más fuertes seamos, más impacto tendremos.*

CONDUCT YOUR OWN REVENUE RISK ASSESSMENT

Become friends with risk by conducting your own revenue risk assessment against the three S's.

- **Sensitivity** – How sensitive is your business to trends? The more sensitive it is, the more likely your bubble is to burst and the more you should pay attention to it. Take action as needed and keep inventory as lean as possible.

- **Simplicity** – How many variations of your core product(s) do you have, or plan to introduce this year? Think about whether or not your product variations are contributing to your revenue growth or confusing the customer into indecision. Ask your employees for their perspective too. Make adjustments to your plan or discontinue as needed.

- **Saturation** – How many new product(s) do you plan to introduce over the next couple years? Did you saturate your market with your current product(s) yet? Determine if you're leaving market share on the table, and potentially overcomplicating your business too early. Review and adjust accordingly.

We know we didn't start this business to get our fifteen seconds of fame and capitalize on trends. We want to build a business that has strong footing in our respective markets to truly impact and disrupt. *¿Estamos listas?*

So much time spent overthinking this decision.
POV: CEO and Founder

Wow, this is hard.

I thought about all the decisions I've had to make as a business owner, but nothing came close to this. Should we enter retailers?

It was on our vision board to take us into retailers, but I didn't know when it would happen. Now that the opportunities were coming, I wasn't sure what to do. I knew it would require so much work. I was comfortable selling online, and we were still growing there, so why not stay? This same loop played over and over in my head the past few years.

The first time we had to make this decision, we went all out. We prepared reports. We did analyses. We reviewed our financials. We had meetings upon meetings, internally and externally. We spent hours thinking about what it could look like. We took a pause on e-commerce initiatives to focus on retailer entry. But in the end, we couldn't do it. There wasn't really a decisive factor that I could point to. I just felt it wasn't time.

The second time we had to make this decision, we did the same thing. Reports, analyses, meetings. But in the end, we couldn't do it. Even though the data pointed to us being able to successfully enter this retailer, I was worried about failing.

The third time we had to make this decision, we did the same thing. For some reason, I wasn't able to move forward. I debated it in my head. I discussed it with my team. I talked about it with other entrepreneurs. I even asked friends and family. But the answer was always no…not yet.

The fourth time, well, we finally did it. And guess what? It went well. We launched and our customers showed up for us. They sold us out during launch week and kept coming back for more week after week. The retailer even spotlighted us several times as a success story. I wondered why I had waited so long. **So much time spent overthinking this decision.**

~

ANALYSIS PARALYSIS

Making decisions as a business owner isn't easy. You make hundreds of them a day. It can feel like there's so much weight on every single decision. *Am I making the right decision? Am I going to be able to make this work? Is this the right investment to make?*

And you should spend time making smart and informed decisions, but there's a fine line between thinking through a decision and overthinking a decision. The latter will cost you. You and your employees spend time pulling reports and attending meetings. The more time they spend on these things, the more you're paying them to overthink with you. So it's not just a time impact, but a cost impact. Not to mention that you're exerting energy going back and forth on the decision.

The risk here is that overthinking and indecisiveness can cause you to wait on opportunities, or spend too many resources on the decision itself, which diverts resources away from other decisions, initiatives, and priorities.

THE STAKES ARE HIGH, ESPECIALLY FOR US

Decisions, and high stakes decisions, specifically, are a special danger zone for overthinking. Entering a retailer is definitely a high stakes decision. It's tricky. You don't want to enter too early or too late. Because sometimes you only get one shot. Your success might also be judged against the same criteria as other established brands that have been there much longer. There are a lot of factors to consider, but don't be a perfectionist. *No lo pienses tanto.*

Do the research, and make a decision whether it's a no, no-revisit, or yes. (A no-revisit means "Let's set it down and move on with other things," a.k.a. it's not sitting on our list of things to think about every week. Give it a three-, six-, or twelve-month horizon.)

Don't shy away from big moves. We tend to wait too long, while others are out there doing it. We often get too caught up in the what ifs, even if the information is telling us to move forward. We already know all eyes are on us, so the fear can be multiplied, causing us to let the opportunity sit for a while until we're able to take the plunge. *¿Qué pasa si es un fracaso?* It won't be if you've assessed your risks!

WELCOME TO THE SÍARM FRAMEWORK

One of the most important frameworks I want to introduce to you in this book is my signature risk management framework that'll empower you to make confident decisions in your business. Whether you're talking about strategy, finances, processes, or large-scale initiatives, it's going to be one of many key enablers you'll have by the time you finish reading this book.

This risk management framework is something that you can easily plug into how you run your business today. Consider it a protective layer that'll allow you to operate your business as the powerful CEO and changemaker that you are.

Do you want to build a beautiful business that grows, scales and impacts?

Hopefully the answer is yes, or *Sí.*

Then **ARM** yourself with a powerful framework, my signature **SÍARM framework**:

- **S is for Strategize** – Strategize what to do and where to take your business. (You already do this!)

- **I is for Identify** – Identify the risks based on your strategy. What are the risks that'll prevent your business from executing on its strategy? Identify what could go wrong, challenges, pain points, etc.

- **A is for Assess** – Assess the risks. Just because things could happen doesn't mean they will, or that you don't already have things in place that'll prevent them from happening. Determine what you have in place to mitigate your risks.

- **R is for Respond** – Respond to the risks based on your assessment. If you don't feel comfortable where you are, do something about it so you can move forward. This could mean implementing a new system or process, hiring someone, or reprioritizing to shift time to this strategy. Take action so you don't leave your business exposed.

- **M is for Monitor** – Monitor your strategy and reassess your risks as needed. A successful business isn't a one and done; it requires constant effort to make sure things are working. Keep an eye on it.

You'll see this framework referenced throughout the book so you can see how it's applied in various scenarios. *Prepárense.*

WHAT'S YOUR BIG DECISION?

What's a big decision you're contemplating making in your business? Maybe one you've been sitting on? Or one you keep revisiting, but can't make a final decision on? Pick one and apply the SÍARM framework to decide if you should move forward.

Chapter 3

Foster a Positive Mindset in Your Employees: Underestimating How Much Your Team Can Affect Your Business Can Leave You Exposed

Y ou didn't think it was just you that needed a risk mindset, did you? Your employees need one too. When your employees know the influence they have, they'll be much more thoughtful about the decisions they make in your business, and you'll be in a much better position to avoid unwanted outcomes and questionable behaviors like product flops, PR disasters, or extravagant spending. In this chapter, we'll discover how to equip your employees with a risk mindset that keeps your business's reputation and resources protected.

I stayed quiet because I didn't think I had any influence.

POV: Sourcing Senior Associate

The plane ride was a bit bumpy, but we made it.

I was still beaming because I was the one selected to go. Me, a Sourcing Senior Associate! I was honored to join our VP of Sourcing as they vetted an international supplier for an upcoming product launch.

For the past two months, we had been planning everything to make the most of our visit. Our sourcing team had put together all the details. The itineraries. The presentations. The timelines. The checklists. And now we were here.

After our delicious hotel breakfast buffet, we took a taxi to the factory to meet the supplier. The entire team was very welcoming. They greeted us with smiles and waves as we walked by, and had coffee and snacks for us in the conference room. We walked through the presentation and timelines with our supplier contact. On our must-have list was all organic materials, and a pretty quick turnaround. They assured us the materials would be available and our short timeline would be fine, even though it was a tight turnaround for our launch date. They showed us samples. By the end of those few hours, our VP was happy and confident that we were in good hands.

All that was left was to sign on the dotted line.

Oh, and a factory tour.

Up until that point, all conversations had taken place in English over the phone with our supplier contact. As we toured the factory, we realized that the workers only spoke Spanish. They stared at us, smiled, and waved, again. They showed us the organic materials, and how they were separate from the other materials so there would be no chance the wrong material was used. However, as we toured, it seemed that the materials were all coming from the same boxes. I didn't see "organic" listed anywhere. I thought it was odd, but figured I just wasn't looking at it correctly. As we were standing at one of the production areas where our VP and the supplier contact were talking, I overheard two of the workers commenting on how there was no way deadlines would be met. Again, I figured they probably didn't know enough. I brushed it off.

*I wish I hadn't. I wish I had said something. Fast forward six months, our timelines were way off and we realized the material was not organic. We weren't able to use the material, and we missed our launch date. **I stayed quiet because I didn't think I had any influence.***

~

HINDSIGHT IS 20/20

First, let's make sure one thing is clear. Being multilingual is a superpower! It should be celebrated, respected, and valued. And whether you speak it fluently, *más o menos*, *un poquito*, or just understand it, know that it's important to our society, to our economy, and to entrepreneurship.

Now, getting into what happened here, you might think, "I would have spoken up." But put yourself in the shoes of a Senior Associate. Their first trip. Their desire to impress. Their goal is to get through the trip and not make waves, unless absolutely certain. And they weren't. They could have put themselves in a bad place if they said something and it was brushed off, or worse—they were reprimanded for it.

EMPLOYEES NEED TO KNOW THEY CAN SPEAK UP

Had the Senior Associate spoken up, it might have prevented this situation from playing out the way that it did. It might have prevented all the headaches that took place over the year of planning for that product launch. You don't want to risk your launches like this!

Employees don't speak up unless they feel like they have approval to do so. Unless they have a safe space to do so. This is why a risk mindset is so important for you *and* for your employees. You want to ensure they know that their opinion is appreciated and should be shared.

Because the reality is you can't have eyes everywhere. You can't make every single decision in your business, especially as you grow and scale. You need the help of your employees to build your beautiful business.

EVERYONE HAS INFLUENCE

Most people build businesses thinking it's only the CEO, top leaders, and heads of departments that have influence. But everyone does. Every single person can protect your business or make mistakes that hurt your business, from the cleaning crew all the way to the CEO. *Todos tienen influencia.*

This is why in all my years as a risk management professional and internal auditor, I always spoke to everyone at all levels when doing risk assessments and conducting audits. You can find out a lot by asking all the right questions to the right people. It helps you keep a pulse on what's happening and what could potentially cause harm to your business.

THANK THEM FOR SPEAKING UP

I still remember clearly the times that employees sent emails about things that seemed off, mentioned something that happened, or called out questionable behavior. It takes courage to do it, and I appreciated the intention behind it. I welcomed it and thanked them for speaking up. *Agradéceles.* Whether they knew it or not, they were using their risk mindset.

You want your employees to keep you informed and you want them to not put you at risk with their decisions, behaviors, and actions. Become friends with risk by talking to your team about the importance of using their risk mindset to identify and speak up about potential risks. *Si les da mala espina*, you want to know about it.

It's all about shaping your risk landscape into what will bring you the most success as you achieve your goals. Your **risk landscape** is the collection of people, processes, and technology, and the risks themselves, that when managed well enable you to achieve your goals, and maximize your impact.

REFLECT ON YOUR RISK LANDSCAPE

The risk landscape you curate matters. How well are your employees equipped to identify risks? Do you ask your employees about risks during meetings or before green-lighting new initiatives? Do you think your employees feel comfortable speaking up? Are there places where you don't have eyes where you wish you did?

I didn't think it would matter, but it did.

POV: Director of Operations

Things were going well at work.

Orders were being placed regularly. Orders were picked and packed efficiently. Orders were delivered to the customer in a timely manner. Our customers were happy. All the five-star reviews proved it. And our people were happy. Everything was operating smoothly like a well-oiled machine. As Director of Operations, that made me feel great.

I was being recognized internally and externally for a job well done. Even outside our internal operations bubble, I was regarded in the industry for my leadership. That year alone I had been invited to speak at several local events and nationwide conferences, and share my best practices. It was part of our strategy for me to be known and recognized for the contributions to our business. I was on podcasts and featured in articles. Everyone would know me and what we did.

Fast forward a few months, I was sitting in my office scrolling on social media apps for a quick brain break. I saw a post about women belonging in the kitchen that I found funny. I reposted it to my page and added a comment reading, "Let's get back to the kitchen, ladies." I didn't really give it a second thought. The next morning, I woke up to a slew of email and app notifications. What was happening?!

The one from my boss read, "CHECK YOUR EMAIL." A glance at my app notifications and all I saw were the words, "jerk," "misogynist," "machista." This couldn't be a good thing. Over the next few weeks, it only got worse. Articles, video commentary, memes—all calling for my demise. The business I worked for was being dragged as well. How could I be such an idiot? I should have known better. But it was done, and it was too late to correct it.

*If the company was going to survive, they had to hold me accountable. I was fired. Never did I expect it to turn out that way, but the writing was on the wall. **I didn't think it would matter, but it did.***

~

NOT ALL PUBLICITY IS GOOD PUBLICITY

In today's environment, people care about what you're saying, doing, and who you're working for, in some instances. While you might be your own person, we're a society, and your views are linked to your ecosystem in one way or another. And while top leaders might be the most visible and easily tied to their business, it applies to everyone at all levels now.

With the internet, anything written, recorded, or filmed is out there—forever.

How many videos have we seen go viral of hatred being spewed by employees, executives, or even professors? I bet right now you can think of at least one instance. I can think of four off the top of my head. An amusement park rant, a distasteful commencement speech, a protest harassment, an insensitive post.

And who do people go after? They go after the company, the organization, the university. The person may not have even posted it directly. But we all know people on the internet are sleuths. They'll find your name, your company, and your title—faster than anything. Once something is out there, it's out there. *Ya no hay quien lo quite.*

If you don't have anything nice to say, don't say anything at all.

DAMAGE CONTROL MIGHT NOT BE ENOUGH

Many companies have resources to do "damage control" on the situation, and likely they fire that person, but you might not be so lucky. You might not have the resources to clear your name, and repair your brand, making it even more imperative that you be proactive when it comes to risk. It could mean the end for your business if it's significant enough.

The truth is you can't afford to lay low for any amount of time because that means you aren't making sales. You still have to move inventory, pay overhead costs, and make payroll. The $$$ needs to come in so that it can be reinvested, keep your business growing, and continue to make an impact. *Tenemos cosas que hacer y gente para ayudar.*

THE SAME GOES FOR SOMETHING CONFIDENTIAL

And while this example is about something negative, the same applies to something confidential. As you grow and scale, you share with your team upcoming changes, product launches, international expansion plans, and earnings results—and you want to ensure that your team knows what can be shared and what's confidential, for internal eyes only.

It's tempting in the beginning to share everything with your team when it's small, but as you expand, you want to make sure you're intentionally sharing what's needed and being clear about what can be shared externally. This isn't about avoiding transparency, but being careful about how well your employees can absorb, handle, and keep the information internal. You want them to understand the implications and err on the side of caution.

I remember once I wanted to post something on LinkedIn, but I knew there was something in there that alluded to something that wasn't yet public. Because I had my risk mindset churning, I consulted with our communications team and ended up removing a couple sentences to make sure my post was in the clear.

You want your employees to be conscious of their decisions, whether that is to post something, not post something, or consult you or someone else before taking action. *Más vale prevenir que curar.*

EMPLOYEES MIGHT NOT EVEN REALIZE

The risk here is that your employees don't know of the repercussions their actions have, and the effect they have on your business—that could even cost them their job. You want your employees to do a double take before saying or posting something negative, or at the very least questionable. Is this something they would be okay going viral for?

And with confidentiality, sometimes they may not even be doing something directly. They may be having an innocent conversation at the airport, or doing work on their laptop in a coffee shop. Maybe they stepped away from their computer without locking their computer screen. They may not be aware of their surroundings.

Even if you have no specific examples for your business, bringing in real-world examples helps employees understand why a risk mindset matters. Their actions have an impact on your business, and especially as you build, you have to protect it. If you instill a risk mindset now, big fires can be avoided. *Evitemos incendios.*

RISK EDUCATION GOES A LONG WAY

This is where proactive risk education comes in. When was the last time you talked to your employees about what can and cannot be shared? How well-equipped do you think your team is to prevent headaches for your business?

Become friends with risk by showing your employees what happens when negative or confidential information is shared. This can be as simple as you talking about it for ten minutes every quarter with a few examples, or taking the time to do risk education training that you prepare, or have an expert come in and deliver.

If you have no formal time to dedicate, you can do it casually. Forward any email examples to your team and say, "Wow! Glad this wasn't <insert your business name here>!" Or say, "I wonder how this happened to them." This will get employees thinking.

It might seem silly, but would you rather spend a few minutes *or* spend a few years—and thousands of dollars—trying to recover your image?

A few parting golden rules to get you started:

- Don't do anything you don't want to see blasted on the news.
- Be aware of your surroundings when talking about your business.
- Close your laptop every time you walk away from it.
- If you're questioning it, you probably shouldn't do it.
- Exercise caution and consult someone if you aren't sure.

I decided to spend now, and ask for forgiveness later.
POV: Product Manager

They were growing fast and they were in need of a Product Manager.

Enter me.

It was what most would consider a stereotypical start-up. Coffee, tea, snacks, catered lunches, and beer on tap. We would go out to lunch, dinner, or happy hour to celebrate milestones, birthdays, or just because. I quickly adapted to their rather lavish ways of spending. Since the team was small and most of the time the founder or a senior leader was with us, we never gave it a second thought as to whether it was allowed or could be considered "too much."

Over the next months and years, our team grew from a team of five to fifteen to fifty, and not everyone could attend every outing. Departments would have their own. Senior leaders would have their own too. I was also promoted to Lead Product Manager, and you better believe every time we launched a product or new collection, we had a celebration. We continued our lavish ways of spending even as we grew, since no one had mentioned otherwise.

One day it was the most gorgeous, sunny day, and many of us happened to be in the office. It was the perfect day for a happy hour. We told anyone and everyone. What started out as an idea between a few people led to a small march through the street on the way to the restaurant. It was a great time with about thirty of us in attendance. We laughed, caught up, and shared stories. You could feel the energy in the room. What started out as one happy hour drink led to a few happy hour drinks. We were so caught up that we didn't even realize when happy hour had ended, and we continued ordering drinks. And after a couple hours, we were hungry and happy, so we started ordering some food. A few of us were even at the point of, "Let's do shots!"

I definitely had the thought that we were probably going a bit overboard, but I told myself it would be fine. It was on the company dime. It had never been an issue before. We were bonding and that's all that mattered. As the night went on, people started trickling out and I became keenly aware that all the spending was on my card. We had racked up a $2,385 bill with countless *drinks, twenty-six shots, several appetizers, and a 25% tip included. I would deal with it later.* **I decided to spend now, and ask for forgiveness later.**

~

A "TREAT YOURSELF" MENTALITY CAN BACKFIRE

Keeping your employees happy and rewarding them for their contributions to your business growth is important. Happy employees, happy business. But you want to make sure that your employees know what you expect from them. What you set as standards of practice is what they'll see as acceptable. It's tempting when you're a team of a few people to go treat yourself, and you should absolutely do it. You work hard, long hours and sometimes it's great to go out and celebrate. It's necessary. But no one needs three cocktails or five shots during an employee happy hour outing. *Claro que sabemos festejar, pero no se pasen.*

I've heard so many conversations between employees who're used to spending excessive amounts because that was how things were done—or that was how the founder did it—so they go wild at happy hours. While this might be a few hundred dollars with a five-person team, once you have a fifty-person team attending happy hours, you end up with a large bill coming your way. I've seen this happen. *Y no les dio vergüenza.*

EXPLAIN WHAT OVERSPENDING MEANS

And this isn't about being stingy, but the truth is every dollar that goes to meals and entertainment is a dollar that you can't reinvest back into your business. Especially for us, those dollars need to stretch as far as they can possibly go. All the *centavitos* are so important as you grow and scale your business. You want your team to treat the business's money as if it was their own.

Employees might not always like you for it, but they'll respect you for explaining what overspending could mean for the business. It could mean you're not able to increase their salaries, grant a bonus, amplify new products, or do a community event that has longer term impacts. Any time you put the alternatives into perspective, employees can get behind the *why*.

YOUR EMPLOYEES LOOK TO YOU

Even if you don't have a specific policy documented around employee spend, your team will naturally look to you for guidance on how to think, act, and make decisions for your business. This is why the behavior you model from the start will inform your employees' behavior. It's also much easier to instill early on versus waiting until it becomes a problem. It's much more jarring to employees who have to make a change. *"¿Cómo que no podemos gastar en esto? Siempre lo hemos hecho."*

The risk here is that employees might acknowledge their questionable actions, but decide it's better to deal with it later after the fact.

You want to think about how you would want your employees to act in these scenarios, as well as any scenario that has risk associated with it. *What does it mean if I make this decision? Is this something my boss would do? Should I ask about it?* And your hope is that if the answer is yes, they should ask, they actually do. They don't keep quiet, or ask for forgiveness later in scenarios where they should have asked up front.

Become friends with risk by modeling the behavior and setting the standard for how you want employees to make decisions. The risk culture you build out will serve you now and into the future.

DON'T AFFECT YOUR BOTTOM LINE

This could seem to some like an extreme example—but these types of reimbursable expenses could wreak havoc on your spend, eat up budget for key initiatives, or affect your profitability, which your investors will definitely have something to say about. And by their nature, these are usually types of expenses that you don't see until after the fact, unless you have all the right processes in place, similar to hotels, flights, photo shoot merchandise, competitor products, and other miscellaneous expenses. Together they could make it harder for you to impact the way you envision.

THINK ABOUT YOUR RECENT SPEND BEHAVIOR

If you think about your recent outings, spend, or business travel, have you exhibited behaviors that you would expect of your employees? Are there any adjustments you can make?

We'll talk more about employee spend in chapter 10, but as a bonus here, if you don't already have one, I'd recommend creating a spending principles document that you onboard employees with, and communicate periodically to ensure employees don't forget. *Para que no se olviden.*

Part 2

STRATEGY

Part 2.6

Chapter 4

Set the Stage with Your Strategy: Lack of Direction Could Take You Off Course

N o business should be without a strategy. When you have a strategy that charts the course for where you want to take your business, you can focus on and prioritize what matters instead of spending time and energy on all the wrong things. In this chapter, we'll walk through how to design an intentional strategy that embeds a risk lens so you can stay headed in the right direction.

I was focused on the wrong things, big-time.

POV: CEO and Founder

I started my day with a cold shower that morning.

Oh well, no big deal. A shorter shower meant I could make it to work a few minutes earlier. I had a full day of meetings ahead and a really long to-do list.

We were doing so many things at once. We were focused on paid ads to help us drive sales. We were working with a PR agency to help us land press features in well-known publications and on TV. We were finalizing logistics for several events we had coming up, including a few conferences, that would increase our visibility. We were adding a new product and a new service that month because our customers were asking for it. We were expanding our team. We were doing what everyone was telling us to do.

Everything seemed to be full speed ahead.

I say "seem" because something felt off.

Maybe it was the cold shower that knocked some sense into me, but my intuition kicked in and got me thinking. Our business was doing well from the outside. We opened it because we believed in what we were doing, and customers quickly believed in us as well. It was go, go, go after that. Sales, PR, product—I did everything I thought we had to.

So why did something suddenly feel off? It all felt wrong.

Why was I doing paid ads even though organic marketing was working just fine? Why did we sign a two-year contract with the PR agency? Why were we attending so many events? Why were we launching a new product and a service at the same time? And what the heck was going on with my back-end operations? It had been months since I talked to some departments and employees. I had always told myself I would build a business intentionally. But here I was, going through the motions to operate a business, without thinking about my strategy. The why behind my decisions. Or the "who" behind my business.

All I knew was I was unhappy. **I was focused on the wrong things, big-time.**

~

IT'S EASY TO GET CAUGHT UP

When we start our businesses, we have an idea of what we want to do and how we want to do it. Then the fun begins. We talk to people. We do research. We go to Google or YouTube University. We join programs, accelerators, and communities.

There's so much guidance coming at us that it's hard not to get caught up in what we think we should do. Either because it's what others are doing, or it's what others are telling you to do. *Add products. Add services. Add marketing and PR. Add people. Add systems.*

And as if that wasn't enough—as your business gets up and running, the day-to-day can start to consume you. We start working *in* our business, instead of *on* our business. (You may have heard this before.) It basically means that you don't have time to think about your big vision anymore. You have to get all of your to-do list done. It's like a web that we get stuck to and as much as we try to escape it, we can't. *Como una telaraña gigante.*

This is why it's critical to chart your direction with a strategy.

WHAT'S YOUR NORTH STAR?

A strategy is your guide to focus on what matters—your North Star. It's your compass. It helps you align your actions with your strategy rather than just take actions for the sake of it. This way you avoid giving attention to things that don't need to be paid attention to.

It makes knowing where to place your precious resources—time, money, and energy—so much easier. It helps you plan your year, make decisions during the year, and have a baseline to assess your progress at the end of the year. It gives you the ability to evaluate, or reevaluate, where you are, especially if you feel like you're veering off path. You want to move the needle toward your North Star, not away from it.

BEING INTENTIONAL WILL TAKE YOU FAR

Beautiful businesses think about their strategy very intentionally. Don't risk spreading yourself everywhere, and going nowhere, due to lack of strategy. You don't want to just go through the motions. Not only do you benefit, but your employees benefit immensely from having a strategy. It helps them know the why behind the business, how to make decisions, and what's expected of them.

Become friends with risk by being clear on what your strategic goals are and your reason for every goal you have. Then, introduce a risk lens to each goal.

FIVE STEPS TO DEVELOPING YOUR STRATEGY

So, how do you build a risk-conscious business strategy? Follow my **five-step strategy blueprint** to set up your business for success.

- **Step 1 – Plan it out.** Do you want your strategy to span over a year, or a few years? When do you want to do it? Who do you want to be involved in it? How will you communicate it to your employees? One year is sufficient as you grow. As you start to scale, you'll want to start thinking a few years out. And from a timing perspective, ideally you're starting to build your strategy in November of the previous year, so that once January comes, you're set to hit the ground running.

- **Step 2 – Pick your core pillars.** How do you think about your business? What do you see as the strategic drivers for your business? Everything you do should fall under one of the pillars. Likely most will in one way or another, no matter the naming you choose to use. Is it customers, employees, stakeholders? Is it sales, product, infrastructure, community? Is it revenue, inventory, operating expenses, innovation? There's no one way to do it. Remember that you're designing *your* beautiful business.

- **Step 3 – Add your goals.** What are the strategic goals you have for your business? What pillar does it fall under? Be clear on exactly why you're adding each goal to your strategy and how it'll move your business forward. Be sure to assign accountability and establish a timeline for each strategic goal. When it comes down to it, each one of your strategic goals will either maintain (e.g., protect), or add value to your business.

- **Step 4 – Add your risks.** What are the risks you're taking on with each strategic goal you've identified? What could go wrong and what do you have in place to make sure it won't? For instance, if you're implementing a new system, the strategic risks are that you pick the wrong one that doesn't align with your business, or that there's a failed adoption of the new system. Think through these risks. With the help of my SÍARM framework you learned in chapter 2, determine if the risks are ones you're ready and willing to take on.

- **Step 5 – Execute on it.** How will you ensure your strategy is being executed? Where will it live? How will you communicate it to employees? Know how you'll effectively track progress toward completion throughout the year. Have one main strategy document and communicate it to your business.

Not every goal has to be about increasing sales. You may be adding goals that require spending money. These can be investments into building your infrastructure, gaining exposure, or building a long-term partnership. You may also be adding goals that save you money. These can be initiatives to optimize inefficient processes or renegotiate with vendors—money which can then be used to invest back in your business.

HOW DOES YOUR STRATEGY MEASURE UP?

Risk and strategy go hand in hand. Review your strategy against my five-step strategy blueprint, and fill in the gaps where needed to curate a risk-conscious strategy for your beautiful business. (And if you don't have a strategy yet, now you know how to build one!)

I tried to do it all at once.
POV: CEO and Founder

I was proud of our business. I was proud of our team. I was proud of how big we were dreaming.

We were going to help our community and make a huge impact. We had a strategy for where I wanted the business to go in the next year.

I was aiming for the stars—expanding the existing product line, adding two new product lines, adding a new channel with retail stores, hiring ten to fifteen people to double our existing team and bring our marketing in-house, and implementing a new CRM system, as well as a financial system. Oh, and we were designing a new office to move into because we were outgrowing our current one.

We had a small team, but we would figure it out. We were smart, talented, and full of ambition. The sky was the limit.

As the year started, we went full force to execute each project. Every month, we would gather the team and do a status update on our strategic initiatives, and initially we felt good about where we were. Everything was in the planning stage.

But a couple months passed and everything was still in the planning stage. I asked about our new product line, and it was stalled because the product team had no bandwidth to review the new designs due to an upcoming launch. I asked about our new retail store research, and it was ready, but no one had time in their calendar to greenlight it to the next step. I asked about our new CRM system, but the IT team was dealing with the implementation of the new financial system. Most of my questions were met with explanations, excuses, or mentions of obstacles.

We talked about it, and everyone said they would make a better effort to move things along. They said it could still get done. Timelines weren't being met, but we could get back on track.

A few months later, we saw some progress.

But as soon as the second half of the year hit, we had other things to deal with, including preparing for a successful holiday season. Everything else slowed again, and by the end of the year, none of our big dreams were carried across the finish line. Not even one. **I tried to do it all at once.**

~

CONNECTING DREAMS TO REALITY

You start your business with a dream. You want to fill a gap in the market, bring innovation to a product or service, or leverage your expertise to serve. You want to make an impact.

And it's okay to dream. It's okay to brainstorm. We should be doing that.

But once you dream as big as possible, it's important to connect the dream with reality for a perfect match. Doing it all at once never works. How many of us have fallen victim to overcommitting? *Somos víctimas de nuestra ambición.*

EVERYTHING ALWAYS TAKES LONGER

It always takes longer than you think. That product you want to design. That proposal you want to send out. That course you want to create. Even those emails you want to draft. You tell yourself it'll take an hour—max two. It'll take four days—max eight. Next thing you know, it's several hours or weeks later, and you've finally done it, but it took ten times longer than you anticipated.

And when it comes to strategy, nothing you put on the list will be a quick execution. Each item will require a significant amount of time and effort. Each one is basically its own initiative that may require multiple team members to provide input, put together deliverables, and implement it. Sometimes we don't realize how much effort something will take, who else needs to be involved in the decision-making process, or who we need help from to execute. We also might find ourselves assuming someone will be able to help us, without thinking about what might be on their plate.

NOT EVERYTHING IS PRIORITY

Become friends with risk by dreaming big, but reining in what can be realistically accomplished. It's important to build a strategy that'll work for your business.

In the last chapter, we talked about creating a strategy because having one is the first step. The next step is to prioritize your strategy. Remove what doesn't belong because when we focus on too many things, we focus on nothing. The risk here is that you take on way too many goals that stretch you and your team too thin, creating a lack of focus on any one thing and an inability to achieve the goals set out, which also leaves your employees feeling confused about the direction of your business.

INVOLVE YOUR TEAM

Once you've done your brainstorming, bring in your team to talk through the strategic goals you've drafted. Not only will this help you gauge what might be too much, but it'll help for your employees to feel part of the process.

You'll get immediate feedback. You'll know who's going to take accountability, or potentially who else will need to be involved. You'll discover where there might be interdependencies that you may have missed. (Interdependencies are where one of your projects has the potential to affect another.)

For example, IT may already have too much on their plate to implement a financial system. And perhaps they weren't even aware of your plans to implement retail stores, which would require them to implement a POS system. Can they do it all? Maybe, maybe not.

Knowing whether they can is the benefit of communicating the strategy before it's set in stone because you'll discover these interdependencies.

Depending on how big your business is currently, there may be a few layers to this process. You can involve everyone at once if you're a smaller team, or you can first meet with department heads, and have them meet with their team.

PRESSURE TEST YOUR STRATEGY

Armed now with the importance of prioritization, review your strategy. Remember that we overestimate what we can do in a quarter, but underestimate what we can do in a year. It's okay to move things around and push things further out. *Date permiso.*

Some strategic goals may immediately need shifting to another quarter, or another year. Some might fall off based on input from your team. Some might have a timeline that's too fast, and need to be adjusted. Some you might realize have too many risks that you aren't prepared for, or ready to tackle.

After pressure testing, you'll have a strategy with three to five main strategic goals, each under their corresponding core pillars. I recommend referring back to them and communicating them to your employees regularly. Doing this will help you evaluate what's most important when other projects, opportunities, or challenges come up during the year. Because they will. *Siempre pasa algo.*

In the end, you'll end up with a strategy that's intentional, manageable, and aligned with you, your team, and your overall vision.

We wasted hundreds of hours.
POV: VP of Strategy

We were going to get it right this year.

This year we would incorporate a more collaborative approach to putting together our strategy, one with employee involvement, and department goals that tied to our overall strategic goals. We had realized there was little input from our employees, and we wanted to change that. We didn't want it to just be the leadership team that developed it.

We wanted the initiative to be led by a professional project manager, so we hired a Director of Project Management. They worked with our strategy team to develop the approach. They designed the process, templates, and timelines. They then worked with our leadership team to develop the top strategic goals based on our core pillars. We assigned the goals to our employees, some who were in the room, and some who weren't. It all seemed to be going well.

After it was ready—or so we thought—the Director of Project Management presented the process to all department heads during the next weekly stand-up meeting. They were instructed to add their department goals into the overarching strategy. We showed them a pretty, colorful table that would serve as the department template. Each department would have two weeks to complete their piece.

Well, two weeks later came. Every template looked different. Every team had added rows and columns where they wanted. What started out as one tweak here and there became impossible to consolidate because it was done as a table on a presentation slide, and not something that could be combined easily. And because we had presented a more condensed version of the deck, some goals we had expected to see in some departments' templates weren't included.

It was so much manual work to try and bring everything together. We had the Manager of Strategy work on it for us, and we ended up with so many slides that could not be condensed in any logical manner. We tried to give guidance on how to update the slides, but the more we tried, the more our department heads and their teams were confused. And we were confused. This *wasn't well-thought-out. Eventually we "tabled it"—a.k.a. gave up. We would proceed with our original strategy document. **We wasted hundreds of hours.***

~

TRASH IN, TRASH OUT

This might seem simple, but it happens all the time. We might have the right intentions to be more collaborative, inclusive, and transparent, but sometimes our process and our templates suck.

There are a few things at play here, but the primary mistake was that the template used to collect the information was ineffective. It would never result in something that was useful to review, monitor, or report out on to management. *Nunca iba a dar resultado.*

Everyone filled out the department template in their own way. Everyone added rows and columns so they could make it work for them. Have you tried to compile presentation tables inside of slides? It doesn't work. It can't be analyzed. It can't be filtered. And ultimately, you can't easily compile tables that come from slides for any type of analysis.

AN INEFFECTIVE USE OF TIME

And yes—maybe if everyone had followed the template perfectly, then maybe the Manager of Strategy could have compiled it into a spreadsheet. But why would you have them waste their time on this manual (and painful) task? Their hours would be better spent on value-add tasks—not copying and pasting information from a slide to a spreadsheet. Start with the spreadsheet!

Remember you're paying your employees for their time, and those *centavitos* need to be well spent.

A QUICK ROAD TO CONFUSION

If you caught it, part of the story also mentioned that goals were assigned to employees that were in the room, and some who weren't. Well, those not in the room were surprised to find out they had goals missing in their department template. If someone isn't in the room, how would they ever know? If your process provides inconsistent or incomplete information, it'll cause a lot of confusion, which could easily have been avoided with better planning.

Unfortunately, in this scenario, however well-intentioned it was, the results were hundreds of hours wasted. *Una desgracia total.*

START WITH THE END IN MIND

So, what could have been done to bring a different, positive result?

Start with the end in mind, and work your way backward. You want an overarching strategy that tells you your top priorities for the year. You want employees to know the top priorities and know how they relate to their specific department priorities. For this to happen, you have to determine how you can weave everything together with a streamlined process and templates that'll serve your business well.

Going about it the right way will put you in the best position to optimize your time, money, and energy, and yield the results you want for your beautiful business. Don't risk executing your strategy with an inefficient process and bad templates! *Terminará en la basura.*

STREAMLINE YOUR STRATEGY

Think about your strategy. What documents, templates, and systems do you use? Is there a way you can streamline it? Is there a centralized location for it? Is there a way you can make it easier for your employees to know their role in carrying it out?

BONUS: TAKE A DEEPER DIVE

On the topic of processes and templates that suck, this is a perfect time to shed light on any areas of your business where your processes and templates might be inefficient, cumbersome, or painful. Make a list, and work with your team to improve them over the next year.

Chapter 5

Each Strategic Objective Deserves Attention: Without Clear Definition, Preparation, and Monitoring, Your Efforts May Prove Unfruitful

Once you have a strategy, it's important to spend time with each of your strategic objectives. Not only do you want to clearly understand what success means and how to get there so you don't waste your efforts, you also want to continuously monitor any factors that could be getting in your way so you can adjust or pivot as needed. In this chapter, we'll talk about how to thoughtfully approach each strategic objective and understand its risks in order to put yourself in the best place to achieve your goals.

I couldn't answer what our KPIs were.
POV: VP of Strategy

Strategy, strategy, strategy.

It's all I had been thinking about and focused on the last few months. "What should the next year look like?" I had all these grand visions, but putting pen to paper proved to be harder than I thought it was going to be. But I did it. I put together a strategy with our CEO that was aligned with our why, and prioritized both what we wanted and could accomplish in the following year.

I was ready to present the strategy to our leadership team. I wanted to get it through final approval so we could show it to all employees at our off-site. This year, it was going to be at a Peruvian restaurant—lomo saltado, ceviches, leche de tigre, causa. I couldn't wait for this year and future years because long term, I had dreams to hold our kick-off meeting in Lima, Mexico City, Buenos Aires, or Quito. But I digress.

I came back from my dreams, and logged on to the meeting with our leadership team.

I presented the strategy, and talked about the goals we would all be striving to achieve that year. "All good," they said. "We see and understand the strategy," they continued. I felt good at that moment.

*Until my Director of Operations raised her hand and asked, "What are our KPIs?" Great question. I was so focused on getting the strategy done that KPIs didn't cross my mind. **I couldn't answer what our KPIs were.***

~

ARE WE THERE YET?

Your strategy might look and feel amazing, but without knowing your **KPIs,** or key performance indicators, you're on a path that doesn't tell you if you've arrived (or are close to arriving). You'll be left asking, "Are we there yet?" So will your employees. *Y queremos llegar.*

This is where KPIs become a partner to your strategy. These indicators are what tell you if your business is achieving its strategy successfully. If you don't have them, it's hard to know if your business is doing well.

For example, if your business has a strategy to improve profitability for your product, what does that look like if executed successfully? Have you identified what profit margin you have now, and what you want to achieve? Are you referring to gross or net profit margin?

Or if your strategy is to improve the customer experience, what does that mean to you? Is it based on the percentage of five-star reviews you have? Is it based on average order value? Is it based on conversion rate? Is it based on return rate?

CONFUSION ALL AROUND

The strategic risk here is that you have a lack of clarity on which performance indicators are important to your business. This can lead to confusion, not only among you and your employees, but also for your board, lenders, investors, or potential investors.

And while we don't get to be a fly on the wall in someone else's business meetings, I'm sure you've seen the episodes of a well-known pitch TV show where some CEOs fumble on what their KPIs are. *Y los tiburones no perdonan.* We don't want to put ourselves in that position. One false move—*y fuera*, at least that's what it can feel like.

YOU CAN'T MANAGE WHAT YOU DON'T MEASURE

The reality is you can't manage what you don't measure. Sounds simple, but a lot of us don't measure KPIs. And even if we do think about them, and maybe even measure them, we don't measure them often enough, or accurately enough.

Become friends with risk by gaining clarity over your KPIs from start to finish, including measuring, validating, and reporting out on them. All these three components work together to form a clear KPI approach for your beautiful business.

So if you're thinking, "I can do a better job with my KPIs," great. Pick your starting point.

If you don't measure KPIs currently: Do your research, and make a list of the ones that apply to your business. There are thousands of KPIs out there to choose from. They can take the form of numbers, percentages, or ratios. If you search for KPIs, you'll find hundreds of articles suggesting which to use. Finance, marketing, product, customers, talent, etc.

But don't get overwhelmed. *Manos a la obra*. Take a wide approach initially, and identify the ones that align with your strategy. Many will seem important, and some may be relevant, but dwindle them down to the ones that move the needle to where you want to go. There might be four that affect how well your marketing dollars are spent, but choose the overarching one that brings all those together.

For instance, going back to the profit margin example mentioned earlier, you might want to improve overall gross profit margin, so it matters how much you're spending on materials, labor, and transportation costs, etc., but the overarching one is your overall gross profit margin. This doesn't mean you don't measure the other ones (more on this below), but these become department level performance indicators that aren't top level KPIs.

If you already measure KPIs (sometimes): If instead you're thinking, "I'm already measuring KPIs," shift your focus to, "Am I measuring them often enough?" Is it part of your regular process? How often do you measure and report out on them?

Go through each of the KPIs you're measuring, and note their frequency. Is it annual, quarterly, or monthly? (Not every one of them needs to be measured at the same frequency.) What frequency will tell you if you're making progress or alert you to make some changes?

Create a reporting dashboard, and save it where you'll be able to access it often and with ease. It doesn't have to be complicated. It can be a spreadsheet. You can fill it in each month for the ones that apply that month, or you can have your team fill it in and send it to you. Then determine who will receive the report every month.

If you already measure KPIs (regularly): If you're already measuring KPIs regularly, then I want you to think about their accuracy. Who's calculating them, and who's accountable for validating their accuracy?

For KPIs to give you a true picture of your business, they have to be accurate. You'd be surprised how many people are basing their decisions on inaccurate information. Someone could be calculating it wrong. Maybe a parameter was entered incorrectly. Maybe it's being pulled carelessly since no one is really checking it. This is where validation plays a part to reduce the risk of relying on inaccurate data, potentially leading to bad business decisions. (Trust me, I've seen it all.)

For example, improving your inventory shrinkage might be part of your strategy this year, and your KPI might be inventory count accuracy. However, you might currently be calculating it based on the actual values with plus or minus values, versus absolute values. Instead of getting an accurate picture of your count accuracy, your pluses and minuses are canceling each other out, misleading you to an inaccurate accuracy percentage.

A QUICK CALLOUT

Un pequeño desvío. Businesses love acronyms. In recent years, there's a new acronym that has emerged and gained popularity: **OKRs**, which stands for objectives and key results. This is another goal-setting methodology, one that's a bit more agile because it focuses on the changes that you want to achieve and it's updated more frequently. Whatever you choose to call it, if you choose to use one or both, the important thing is that you identify and measure your strategic goals. Start somewhere and go with it. *No te hagas bolas.*

REVIEW YOUR KPI APPROACH

If you think about your KPI approach, do you have one? Have you identified the top level KPIs that'll indicate your performance? Do they align with your strategy? How confident are you with their accuracy? How often do you report out on them, and to who? Is it your team, your board, or your investors?

I'd recommend having around five KPIs, no more than ten. Any more than that and you'll spread your attention too thin, and it'll divert attention away from what matters.

BONUS: TAKE A DEEPER DIVE

As you grow and scale, you'll want to incorporate tiers for your KPIs so that everyone stays connected to the bigger picture even as your team expands and becomes more decentralized.

For instance, from the top level KPIs, you could extend into department level and/or employee level tiers. This would enable each department and employee to know exactly how their work fits into the overall success of the business. And it also would ensure that responsibilities are clear so that every department and employee can be accountable to what they need to deliver. (Employee level KPIs are great to incorporate into performance plans.)

Bueno. Have you had it with the word KPIs? Me too. *Pasemos página.*

We were doing so well and then we weren't.
POV: Director of Sales

I was ecstatic, to say the least. We were in a huge growth phase.

Month after month, our sales had continued growing. We didn't think we would outpace the prior month, but we did. We weren't sure if our new launch would be a hit, but it was. We weren't sure if our partnerships would work, but they did. Despite an incredibly difficult economy, we were doing better than many industries and most businesses.

The world was our oyster. There was no end in sight. "To infinity and beyond!" our team would say during meetings. They were used to seeing sales, but this was to another level. We felt unstoppable to be honest. We started investing in more people, more technology, and more resources. We hosted more employee events and off-site retreats. We became much more generous with employee gifts.

We didn't think it would slow—but it did.

It slowed a bit at first. Then faster. And faster.

We realized something had changed. We realized spending habits were changing. We realized people were attracted to what we had to offer when they spent more time at home due to a certain situation we won't speak of, but once that turned around, they weren't shopping with us anymore.

Our happiness came crashing down when sales slowed, and we were forced to update our financial projections. They now looked bleak. The balloon had burst and we were deflating. ***We were doing so well and then we weren't.***

~

NO ONE IS UNTOUCHABLE

There are times when running a business that being slightly delusional works. *Feliz como una lombriz.* We need the confidence, adrenaline, and faith in ourselves, and our team. We face a lot every day, but we shouldn't underestimate how fast things can change. And we should never cross into the territory of thinking we're untouchable.

Even if your strategy is to grow, grow, grow, and you might set off on that path, it doesn't mean things won't change unexpectedly. Some things are outside your control. *No puedes controlar todo.*

FOR BETTER OR FOR WORSE

When thinking about strategic risks, it's not just enough to think about all your internal factors (e.g., production, sales, fulfillment). The external factors matter just as much. What's going on in the economy? What's the government doing? What's the media covering? For better or worse, external factors could affect your business trajectory.

But when you have a risk lens, you back the confidence you're feeling and seeing in your results with thoughtful preparation, analysis, and monitoring. *Estarás preparada y lista para lo que sea.*

UNDERSTAND YOUR EXTERNAL FACTORS

Knowing where you stand will give you incredible insight into your business.

Become friends with risk by understanding your sales growth and keeping up to date with key external factors and changes.

If you're considering macroeconomic factors regularly, you'll be aware about possible economic changes coming your way. Is revenue up because the economy is doing well in your specific industry? What could cause it to swing another way?

If you're considering government actions regularly, you'll know about potential regulation changes that could affect you. Is your profit healthy because there's a rebate or tax break you're benefiting from? Is it temporary? If so, when does it expire? Is it possibly going to change in the next election?

If you're considering the media coverage regularly, you'll be able to identify shifts in public perceptions as early as possible. What themes are you seeing being covered in articles, on TV, or on social media? Is your product booming because of something specific? How likely is that to shift?

You want to be aware and prepared. It's all about understanding the part your business plays in the current ecosystem. Especially as your product or service is new and establishing itself, don't rely on instant success to always be the norm. It'll take years to establish staying power. Until then, identify which signs you'll pay attention to. Think about it like a pendulum. What will cause it to swing wildly? What type of swing are you comfortable with? Then, plan for the worst, and hope for the best.

HOW WILL YOU KEEP A PULSE?

Have you considered how external factors affect current growth, and could affect planned growth? Determine which external factors could affect your growth and how you'll keep an eye on them. Consider alternative scenarios, develop backup plans and adjust your strategy as needed.

And you don't have to do it all yourself. Enlist the help of your employees by assigning each external factor to the most appropriate person. Hold them accountable for knowing and reporting up what you need to know, whether they present it every quarter, bring it up during your one-on-one, or communicate it at a leadership retreat.

BONUS: TAKE A DEEPER DIVE

Once you scale to seven figures, protect your business with an enterprise risk management program, also known as ERM. This is a formal program where you identify, assess, and monitor your top risks to prevent negative business outcomes. Typically, it would be managed by an ERM program lead, and possibly a small team, though the ownership of knowing the risks, and reporting out on them, would be within the business (e.g., you would assign each one to someone in your business, typically a department head). This is great to consider once you're ready to dedicate even more resources to protect what you're building.

So much time dedicated to expanding, and it flopped.
POV: VP of Strategy

So many dream of taking their business international.

Everyone always asked us if we were going to. We always answered with a "No, not yet."

After a few years, we decided it was time.

Instead of expanding to the EU as most did, we decided to start in the UK first because it was a large market with plenty of potential.

It was going to be great. Our product was such a success here, why wouldn't it be there? We assembled a team, and picked a code word for the project: Other. Mostly because in the UK they drove on the other side of the road. We approved the timeline, budget, and initial head count. We started doing market research, and made a few trips out there. Things were in motion. We hired our General Manager and Customer Service team. We found our local distribution center.

Meanwhile in the US, our teams who would incorporate the UK into their roles—product, sales, marketing, engineering, IT—were hard at work. The majority of them had no experience with the UK market, and relied heavily on their knowledge of how to do things for the US market. We did hire subject matter experts to help in some areas, but for the most part we figured it would be a lift and shift. What was working here should work there. We did take some precautions, for instance with inventory where we selected only a specific set of SKUs that would be available in the UK.

About two years later, after a lot of sleepless nights, we were ready to launch. Our website was ready. Our distribution center had inventory and was ready to ship. Our marketing plan was ready. Our customers were hopefully out there.

Go live day came, and we launched! Our first sale came in! Our second sale came in! We were doing it. We had a launch party, and gave a special gift to everyone on the launch team. The office buzzed with excitement. We were now international, and no one could stop us.

A few months went by. We looked at the data, and we realized that our first-time customers weren't converting. They were taking the launch discounts and gift cards, using them, and not coming back. We expected it, but not to this extent. We also thought new customers would come in. We had invested significant dollars in paid ads, and plastered our brand on billboards all over the UK. And while we saw some returns and increased brand recognition, it wasn't enough.

When we looked at how much we invested versus how much we made, it was far from a success, but maybe we needed to wait it out a bit longer. So we waited. And waited. After several months of losses, we called it quits. **So much time dedicated to expanding, and it flopped.**

~

THE SAME RULES MIGHT NOT APPLY

There are a lot of things where I would say go for it. *¡Échale ganas!*

Expanding internationally isn't one of them. This undertaking requires thoughtful planning, intentional decision-making, and careful execution. It requires so much time. And money. *Mucho dinero.*

It's great to have ambitions of expanding internationally. Many do, but sometimes we think that because we're doing so well in our domestic market, there's no reason they wouldn't love us in another country. Sometimes we think we can simply "lift and shift" our existing operating model to the new country. Sometimes we think, "It'll all work itself out eventually if I work hard at it." But there are so many nuances to operating in a new country that you have to pay attention to. It's impossible to know everything, so we owe it to ourselves to do our due diligence.

We have to know if our products will do well there, and which ones will do well. We have to lean on those in the market to guide us. We have to have a clear understanding of how much investment this will take and when we aim to turn a profit.

The risk here is that you don't do enough market research and testing before entering a brand-new market, especially when going abroad. I don't want you to experience what they did in this story. *Sería una pesadilla.*

DON'T SKIP OUT ON PREPARATION

For big moves like this, you need to make sure there are enough customers who're interested in your product before going through the entire effort of launching internationally. Test, test, test.

Start small and slow as you learn the market. This could look like doing pop-up stores, expos, or markets. This could look like working with a retailer in a few of their stores. You could do focus groups. You could build a social media presence first and generate buzz through a pre-sale list. You could even start just by shipping internationally. It's much easier to do a few $25,000 tests than to invest a few million dollars and fall flat on your face. *No queremos eso.*

You want to make sure you're undeniably ready to expand internationally. You know the market, you know the people, you know how you'll gain traction. You know how you'll make sales, and turn a profit. You know how you'll run back-end operations.

Become friends with risk by strategically expanding into new markets *after* thoroughly researching options and considering all the parts that'll bring you success. Because with these types of strategic initiatives, you risk more than just your investment. You risk your reputation as a leader and as a business. You should do everything in your power to be prepared. *Preparadita te ves más bonita.*

ASSESS YOUR STRATEGIC RISKS

We're applying the principle of being prepared to expanding internationally, but the same goes for expanding product lines, channels, etc., and any kind of strategy that'll cause a significant shift in your business and will require $$$ to undertake. Don't wing it, and hope for the best.

You already know what I'm going to say—assess your risks! Every strategy deserves a risk lens. What will happen if anything and everything goes wrong? Will you, your business, and/or your board be okay with it?

And of course, you'll never be 100% ready, or know 100% of what the outcome will be. That's not the objective. The objective is to take on the level of risk that you and your business are okay with. You're taking on some level of risk by going after big goals (remember upside risk from earlier?). You have to determine what levels of experimentation are comfortable for you: a lot, a little, or somewhere in between.

MASTER THE HMMM STRATEGY APPROACH

When I was writing this chapter, I pictured powerhouses sitting around a conference room. Amazing ideas flying. *Let's do this. Let's do that. Ooo that's a great idea. Ooo that one too. What should be part of our strategy?* After narrowing the ideas down to a few, you're ready to plug in your risk lens. You say, "Hmmm… Are we ready?"

Apply the **HMMM strategy approach** to decide if a particular strategy will work for you before you embark on execution. It'll save you time, money, and energy in the long run.

- **H is for Home** – Does this strategy fit in with your ethos, your values, and your vision? Does it help you move toward your North Star? We can easily fall victim to shiny object syndrome if we aren't careful.

- **M is for Market** – Is the market ready? No doubt you have a great product, but is the market ready for what you have to offer? Is your brand going to be received well? Is your current market ready for you to move on? Are you close to being saturated? A lot of times we try too many things too fast. Keep it as simple as possible for as long as possible. As long as you're growing, what's the rush?

- **M is for Money** – How much money will it take? What will you make? What discounts will you offer? What are your expenses? What are the big investments you'll have to make up-front? Can you phase them in? For instance, by waiting to open the distribution center and absorbing some of the shipping costs initially, you could save money before going all in.

- **M is for Management** – Are your people, existing or to be hired, ready to manage the execution? Can they absorb the additional work? Sometimes we assume it's the same type of work—but it's a whole new country! For example, accounting has a handle on payments in your country, but handling payments in another country is an entirely new setup with new bank accounts and accounting records.

So next time you have a brilliant idea, I hope you think HMMM.

WHAT SIGNIFICANT SHIFTS DO YOU HAVE IN YOUR BUSINESS?

What are your top three strategies for this year, or the next few years? Are you ready, or do you have a plan in place to be ready? Apply the HMMM strategy approach and see where you land. Make adjustments as needed. Keep yourself on track to build your beautiful business!

Chapter 6

Cultivate a Strong Culture: Disengaged Employees Will Not Execute Your Strategy Well

Y ou can have the greatest strategy in the world, but if your employees aren't motivated to execute your strategy, you won't go as far. When you prioritize creating a culture with open lines of communication, quality talent, and safe spaces, it'll pay you back multiple times over, and you'll avoid having disengaged, unhappy employees. In this chapter, we'll address how you can cultivate a strong culture that doesn't put your strategy at risk, one with employees that are aligned with your strategy, and ready to execute it well.

As long as leadership knows, I think I'm good.
POV: CEO and Founder

I was burning the midnight oil.

Not because I had worked a really long day, but because I was a night owl, and inspiration had struck. It was strategy season, and I had been working on our strategy for a couple weeks. It was coming together nicely. I knew what would happen in each quarter. I was spacing things out nicely too. Not like last year when I thought I could get everything done in the first quarter. We get so excited, you know. This year, I was still excited, but I was much more realistic. My excitement would be contained to what our business could handle.

As I set up our strategic goals and aligned them to their respective core pillars, I pictured the person or the team who would execute it. In the next couple days, I finalized the strategy and discussed it with my leadership team. I assumed each leader would communicate it to their team, including assignments as applicable.

What I didn't know was that some leaders would send it to their teams via email, some would present it during a team meeting, and some would sit down with each person individually.

Later I also found out that some had slipped through the cracks, either because they were caught up in another meeting, or were out of office that day.

But I'm getting ahead of myself.

Rewind a few days. I asked our Customer Success Associate how they felt about the changes that were coming this year. They replied, "What changes?" I had this image in my head of how the customer success team was going to optimize our customer experience, but they had no idea. Later I ran into the Customer Success Manager, and they had no idea either. This theme continued throughout the day with other teams.

*Was anyone as excited as I was about our strategy? I guess not, because they didn't even know about it. My misguided belief had failed me. I falsely assumed: **As long as leadership knows, I think I'm good.***

~

DON'T ASSUME EVERYONE IS ON THE SAME PAGE

I'm sure you've heard the saying, don't assume—it makes an a** out of you and me. It's not enough to have a strategy that you know and love. You need to ensure that you effectively communicate it to your business. Because with strategic goals comes strategic communication. They should know your strategy—what it is, what it means, and what role they play in it. This way everyone is on the same page, and moving toward the same goals. What good is a well-thought-out strategy if your employees don't know about it? *Que no sea en vano.*

BAD COMMUNICATION WILL DAMAGE YOUR CULTURE

With something as important as your strategy, it's crucial that you find the right avenues to communicate it because bad communication around your strategy can damage the culture you aim to create. Employees want to feel in the loop, not out of the loop. They don't want to be confused or surprised.

And while it's normal to lean on your leadership team as you grow since you can't be everywhere at once, you'll still want to set up multiple communication methods to make sure everyone knows what your strategy is. It could be a weekly stand-up, an all hands, a town hall, or an email, depending on how your business is organized.

Whichever communication method you choose, make sure there's also enough time for employees to digest the information and ask questions. Otherwise you risk creating a disconnect, which will ultimately foster a culture of miscommunication, or a lack of transparency. The last thing you want is to affect your culture, or for your strategy to be left open to interpretation.

OVERCOMMUNICATION IS KEY

Become friends with risk by always communicating—even overcommunicating—with your employees regarding your strategy. If your strategy lives rent-free in your head, or in a document that only you have access to, then it's not serving you well. Employees can't read your mind!

You *can* have a beautiful business with everyone feeling they're an important part of it. To achieve this, as much as possible, allow your team to be part of the strategy creation process and walk them through what you're thinking and envisioning. Talk about the thought process and purpose behind each strategic goal, as well as who's assigned as accountable for it. The more they can understand where you're coming from and the more they understand which pieces they're responsible for, the more they can get on board. This will inform their day-to-day decisions and actions because they'll know if something is, or isn't, moving your business forward. And this way, you don't risk your employees making their own goals and priorities that don't align with your business strategy.

The more you can communicate, the better. And this goes beyond just communicating when you first create the strategy. Keep your employees informed every so often—monthly, quarterly, or biannually.

I know it's cliché, but communication really is key. Nothing is more powerful in helping you prevent challenges as you build your beautiful business than communication. I can't stress this enough.

REFLECT ON HOW WELL YOU COMMUNICATE YOUR STRATEGY

If you reflect on your strategy, does everyone on your team know it, or do you just think they know it because you do? How often are you sharing progress? Are you updating your employees if you make changes? And are there any specific instances that come to mind when looking back where you now realize there was a lack of communication?

Find easy ways to ensure open and consistent communication with your employees whether that's via a central strategy document that's accessible to all team members or through monthly emails. You can even gamify it so your employees have fun ways to remember key parts of your strategy.

My business was growing fast, so I had to hire fast, right?

POV: CEO and Founder

Until this year, we had a small team that worked well together.

We genuinely wanted to know how each other's day was. We ate lunch together regularly, and we knew about each other's lives. We communicated well, and got sh*t done. Maybe we could have stayed like that for a while, but we had grown so much in the past year. It was time to hire.

We set up a super thorough hiring process. Each candidate met with HR first, followed by a slate of interviewers, including their possible boss, their possible boss's boss, and any key stakeholders they would be working with. Each new employee also had a comprehensive onboarding process. This worked well for the first half of the year. We had the cash to invest, and we wanted to build out our team to scale. Because we had the time, we dedicated ourselves to hiring great candidates.

But as sales skyrocketed, we started dedicating our attention elsewhere. We hired, but started paying less and less attention to who as long as they seemed alright and it got the hiring to-do off our plate. We started interviewing candidates that weren't qualified, and we spent double the time training the decent ones we let slip through. Many times we ended up filling the same role a second time instead of searching for the right person the first time. It was a disaster.

What hurt us even more was seeing our culture shift. We ended up losing some of our original team because they didn't like the new hires, or the new environment they created. All I kept thinking in my head was: **My business was growing fast, so I had to hire fast, right?**

~

CUTTING CORNERS WILL BACKFIRE

Hiring is likely in your strategy and rightfully so. There are only so many possible clients you can talk to, social media posts you can prepare, and orders you can fulfill on your own. Your capacity is limited and our capabilities are not all-encompassing.

Once it comes time to hire, a lot of questions come up. *What roles should I hire for? Where am I at capacity? What do I not like doing? Who do I hire? How do I hire? Will I hire the right person? Can they do it as well as me?* (I'd venture to guess a lot of us are recovering perfectionists.)

It's hard to delegate, and it'll take time, so let's not make it harder on ourselves by messing up the hiring process once we do take the plunge. In this scenario, the hiring process was actually designed well, but failed in its execution.

The hiring process isn't something you want to cut corners on because it'll have consequences for your overall business.

HOW YOU HIRE WILL IMPACT YOUR BUSINESS

Not hiring and retaining quality talent is one of the top risks you'll face in your business. It's a strategic risk that you have to identify and manage, or else it'll affect your culture—whether you know it or not. So think about it, *por favor.*

Here are a few pieces of advice to think about.

Don't waste time interviewing unqualified candidates. Maybe they didn't get hired in the end, but even letting one unqualified candidate go through even part of the process wastes hours of time that can be spent elsewhere.

I have vivid memories of one specific candidate that I interviewed that wasn't qualified, and couldn't care less about being considered. The entire interview all I could think was, "What am I doing here? Why did I spend time preparing for this interview, and why did talent acquisition send this person through?" And they had two other interviews scheduled, which meant that they were going to waste the time of other employees too. (In an effort to save others' time, I tried to wave a flag, but I was overruled. Guess what! They felt the same way I did after their interviews.)

Putting this into perspective, the three of us took time out of our day to prepare, interview, and log our completed interview into the system. Even conservatively saying this was two hours each, that's six hours of time your employees could have used elsewhere. Six hours of time you paid them to waste. Not to mention that each time you switch tasks, it takes time for your brain to readjust and get back into focus mode. This is a perfect example of how to waste time in your business. Don't interview *quien sea. ¡No seas mensa!*

Don't hire just to hire. Hiring just to hire only provides short-term relief to allow you to fill the role. You might have been tired of waiting, tired of interviewing, and thought, "Hey this person's good enough." But what happens? You'll end up spending so much time training them. And in many cases, they do the job for six months, a year maybe, and leave. Putting this into perspective, you spent hours hiring, onboarding, and training this person. It's such an inefficient use of resources, and we don't have resources to spare!

Don't hesitate to fire fast. "Hire slow, fire fast," is a typical phrase you hear when it comes to hiring, which essentially means take your time to hire. Who you hire will affect your business and its culture, so it's worth it to dedicate time and energy to hire intentionally. And if you do find someone is negatively affecting your culture, fire fast. Pull them out of your ecosystem quickly. *Como una mala hierba.*

Don't forget to think about culture. Every time we hire, we adjust our culture. Great hires will enhance your culture and contribute positively to it. Bad hires will affect culture in a negative way, making it harder to maintain the culture you have worked so hard to build. Believe it or not, employees will leave if they notice a culture shift they aren't aligned with. Employees are very observant and notice more than you think. They notice if you go from hiring top talent to mediocre talent. They also notice if you used to value life-work balance, but now are hiring people who want to work around the clock.

For instance, if you have a culture of great life-work balance and avoiding burnout, but then you hire someone who mentioned doing whatever it takes, and being willing to put in the late hours, this can affect your culture. Instead, put pressure on them during the interview to expand on that, and don't be afraid to be up-front about it. They might really feel that way, or they might be answering the way they think they should answer. Either way, you find out if they would be a good addition to your team. (Speaking from experience, in one instance I found that this happened, them answering the way they thought they should, and I was hesitant to make sure they truly felt this way. I'm so glad I listened to my gut and had them clarify. They were a great hire and I almost passed on them.)

DISCUSS HIRING PLANS WITH YOUR EMPLOYEES

As much as it's about who you're bringing on, make sure those you have on board are ready. Once you're ready to hire, have honest conversations with your current employees about who you plan to hire and your expectations for what that'll look like. It'll allow for a much smoother transition if your team can see your vision and help you onboard your new employees.

¡Aguas! For many of us, we lean on the generosity of family and friends to help us out initially, and they may be some of our first employees. When it comes time to expand to non-family and friend employees, you especially want to make sure they're aware that things may look different as you enter your new phase.

Your mom might be used to coordinating the packing of orders, but now you want the experienced person you hired to take it over. You and your friend might be used to talking casually and telling inside jokes during your work meetings, but now you want your meetings to be more focused and want to be seen and respected as a leader. Or you and your partner might be used to making all the decisions together, but now you want to be more inclusive and consult others.

Even if it feels awkward to have the conversation, openly talking about what changes to expect can prevent a lot of hiccups down the road. *Solo buenas vibras.* Remember you're running a business here. Ultimately, you want everyone to understand that hiring is a good thing and everyone will benefit from it.

LEVERAGE ALL OPTIONS FOR SOURCING TALENT

Don't feel pressure to hire full-time employees right away! If you aren't sure or don't want to commit, hire a consultant or contractor to see how they do. We're in an amazing landscape now where there are a lot of boutique consulting firms, agencies, fractional businesses, and freelancers, ready and willing to support you. This gives you a great opportunity to support business owners that are aiming to impact just as much as you are.

EXECUTE YOUR HIRING STRATEGY

Once you're ready to add hiring to your strategy, determine why, when, how, and who you'll hire. And if you're already hiring, think about how these principles are incorporated.

Why? You should be hiring either to increase capacity or increase capabilities. Determine which hires you need to move your business forward and be clear what purpose each hire serves.

When? The hiring process takes time away from other activities. There's no way around it, so make sure you and your team are ready for it. Weigh other priorities and make sure everyone is okay with what will slow down because of the time it'll take to hire and onboard.

How? It's worth it to have a candidate interview with the few key people they'll be working with, not just those who rank above them. Identify the appropriate slate of interviewers and refine the slate as needed. Be thorough, but also don't go overboard.

Who? We used to all be focused on hiring for cultural fit, but fit implies we're trying to hire someone who fits a mold. We're disruptors after all and we're hiring to change the existing narrative and become more inclusive because we know the power it has. True cultural alignment is someone who will *add* to the culture.

Become friends with risk by implementing a thoughtful strategy for hiring that considers the time and resources spent on interviewing, including which caliber of candidates should interview in the first place. And remember to look for culture alignment in a holistic way.

We were unhappy and our boss had no idea.
POV: IT Manager

They knew the team was getting ready to head out, but they didn't care.

As sunset approached, our boss pinged everyone with the dreaded "Do you have a minute?" and called us into a meeting. We all assembled and took our seats with confused looks on our faces. We could tell something was wrong.

They finally spoke. "You all need to do better," they said. "I expect more from every single one of you," they yelled. We could tell they were fuming. "How can I trust you to do anything if this is the work you turn in?" they continued. It almost reminded me of a child who was in tantrum mode. We all just sat there, unable to speak. After a few minutes of silence, one of us raised our hand and asked how we could do better. "I don't know, just do better," they said.

Not for lack of trying, but for a few months now, we had felt like whatever we were doing wasn't enough. It was a tension that had continued to build, evidently until this moment.

It wasn't always like this.

They actually used to be a great communicator with a "my door is always open" and "we're one team" attitude. But it seemed that the more we grew and the more there was to do, the more they morphed into a new person who didn't know how to communicate well and was always stressed. They would never admit that though.

Ironically, they would tell you that they were great at communicating and listening. But we learned our lesson a few months ago when we finally got them to do a 360-feedback process thinking it would provide us with a space to speak up in an anonymous setting. It didn't. In fact, they thought that we were going to give feedback to each other and not to them, so they didn't even read the feedback. After that, we knew things probably weren't going to change.

And now this. What would they do next?

We didn't know but we weren't going to stick around to find out. It was time to start our exit plan. **We were unhappy and our boss had no idea.**

~

DON'T SCHEDULE IMPROMPTU MEETINGS, PLEASE

Scheduling an impromptu meeting at the end of the day is a surefire way to make your employees freak out. *¿Quién metió la pata?* It diverts their focus from what they were working on, and becomes the only thing they can think about.

And if you call an unexpected meeting, the last thing you want is to express anger. It's something your employees can't unsee, and will for sure talk about after the meeting is over. Have you ever exploded in front of your friends or family, and regretted it? It happens. We're all human. As a leader, your employees want you to be human too, but there's a certain amount of level-headedness they need. You set the tone. You set the example. They look up to you. Don't underestimate the effect of a "cooldown" whether it's alone, or with confidants.

Schedule the meeting once you're ready, and once your employees are ready. (Not right before the end of day, *por favor.*) Headspace matters.

RETAIN YOUR TALENT WITH A STRONG CULTURE

When you own a business, your work as a culture architect is never done.

Your actions affect how employees think about their environment, how they act within it, and whether they decide to stay. They watch, absorb, and notice what you do and how you approach situations. They'll mirror it in some cases. It's a lot of pressure, no doubt. But if you want a beautiful business, inside and out, it's something you want to wrap your head around fast. Because your culture extends beyond the mission and vision you have on your website. It's the day-to-day that your employees experience and what keeps them motivated.

Happy employees will be engaged, productive, and excited to help you. If they leave, you can't achieve your strategy. (Remember when we talked about how not hiring and retaining quality talent is one of your biggest strategic risks? This is the retention part.)

Always remember that culture isn't a "set it and forget it" type of thing. Keeping a strong culture is something you have to actively work toward every day.

A SAFE SPACE TO SPEAK UP

One of the most important elements of a strong culture is a safe space for open communication. You want employees to feel comfortable speaking up. You want them to be able to bring up any problems to you. And you want to know if they're unhappy!

From the time you hire your first employee, your strategy should include a thoughtful approach as to how you'll create your safe space where you and your employees can voice their thoughts, opinions, and concerns. Safe spaces ensure your employees feel seen, understood, and valued—and they're critical to maximizing your impact.

And of course, there'll be times when you want to talk to your employees about hard, challenging topics. When this happens, just make sure you think through your messaging and how you want things to be received. (Not like they did in this story, *obviamente*.)

AVOID CREATING A NEGATIVE CULTURE

I don't think anyone actually sets out to create a negative culture, but it can inadvertently happen over time. Especially with mounting responsibilities, pressures, and overwhelm, it can be hard to keep the same approach or demeanor you had when you started your business. And that's *exactly* why you want to pay extra attention to how you communicate and why you want to keep a pulse on how employees are feeling in your business.

Because as your employees observe your culture negatively changing over time, they'll start to become disengaged. For instance, employees will notice if you play favorites, put unrealistic pressures on your team, allow unfair situations, or tolerate microaggressions, etc. Instead of talking about aspirations, ambitions, and business goals, they start whispering about you and what's happening. (This is the kind of *chisme* you don't want.)

The reality is they can only stay for so long in a negative environment. While most employees will give you some grace at first, they'll eventually start crafting their exit strategy, which can be immediate or can take years. They may "quiet quit" first, which means they stop caring about your business. So even though they show up every day, they aren't delivering anymore. They may become so disgruntled that they request a sick leave, or find ways to take from your business, a.k.a. fraud. Plus, one employee's attitude and behavior can easily affect other employees, and that might mean you start to see more absenteeism, low morale, and lack of trust in your overall workplace.

IS YOUR CULTURE ALL TALK?

Become friends with risk by establishing a culture that isn't just talk or theory, but shows up in action.

What culture do you have in your business? Do you have a set of values that's the heartbeat of your business and do your employees embody it day-to-day? Do you communicate well? Do you have trust in the workplace? Do you listen to employee concerns with an open mind? Whether it's a team of two or a team of one hundred, determine how you'll ensure a strong culture, and how you'll notice shifts.

BONUS: TAKE A DEEPER DIVE

Especially as you expand your team, be aware of silos and microcultures that'll naturally show up as you grow into multiple departments. You'll now have to rely on the department managers to keep the culture strong and aligned day-to-day. Whereas you might have previously been able to say hi to everyone and know their lives, you now might only really see and interact with your immediate team. It'll become important to find other avenues to keep your rapport intact—possibly with periodic check-ins, office hours, employee surveys, or a 360-feedback process.

A 360-feedback process can be an effective tool to promote safe spaces and speak-up culture. If you hear your team start asking for a 360-feedback process, it's likely a sign that many have an issue with their boss or boss's boss, or a colleague, or maybe even you, and they don't feel comfortable expressing this directly.

A word of caution though: I've seen businesses go through a 360-feedback process, and ignore the feedback given for leadership. (Sometimes leaders tend to think that because they have a big, fancy title, or because they've had a twenty-plus-year career, nothing is wrong with them.) But we can all learn from each other, no matter our age, title, demographic, education, or experience. So make sure you take the feedback seriously.

Part 3

PROCESSES

Chapter 7

Document Your Processes for Peace: Keeping Everything in Your Head or Up to Chance Will Breed Overwhelm and Confusion in Your Business

P rocesses are a playbook of your business operations. By dedicating time to documenting your processes, you release the burden of keeping everything in your head or up to chance, and you significantly reduce the effects of an employee leaving or unknowingly duplicating work with another employee. In this chapter, we'll discover how documenting your processes helps you steer clear of risks that could slow you down so you can enjoy freedom, protection, clarity, and peace—all critical elements of a beautiful business.

My brain needed some oxygen.
POV: CEO and Founder

"Today is going to be a busy day," I said to myself.

But then again—I think I said this every day.

The list was long. We had online orders to fulfill for our latest sold-out launch. We had wholesale orders to fulfill. We had a ton of vendor invoices to process so we could get our vendors paid on time because we'd been having some issues recently. We had marketing assets to create. We had two new hires to onboard. We had investor presentations to prepare. I felt stressed just thinking about everything that had to get done.

Starting from the top of the list, I sat with our Ecommerce Assistant to review the online orders. I walked them through all the validation checks that needed to be made as part of the process on quantities, SKUs, and addresses to ensure everything was fulfilled correctly. Next, I sat with our Wholesale Supervisor to review wholesale orders for each retailer—a manual and rather tedious process because each retailer had their own nuances. And because I forgot how to add wholesale partners to the system, we spent extra time figuring out how to add them.

I snuck in a quick coffee refill to refuel me before working with our Accounting Analyst to input all invoices into the system. I showed them how to set up the due date correctly, and set some time aside to review it later in the week. After that, I didn't have the energy to explain to our Marketing Associate how to create marketing assets, so I canceled the meeting. I would prepare them myself. It would be faster that way. By the time I got to onboarding, I was exhausted. And of course, I forgot to coordinate their schedules, so I felt like a broken record explaining everything twice. Plus, I realized after that I forgot to cover company confidentiality with one of them. One more item for the to-do list...

It was a mess. It all got done, but at what cost? I felt overheated.

Everything relied on me to get across the finish line because I had the knowledge and the nuances in my head. There had to be a better way. I didn't even get to the investor presentations, which I'd been pushing back for weeks now. Why did I do this to myself? **My brain needed some oxygen.**

~

YOUR BRAIN NEEDS SPACE TO BREATH

A seemingly never-ending to-do list... I'm sure you can relate.

As an entrepreneur, you start out with all the excitement of building your business and bringing your vision to reality, but you quickly find yourself bogged down with tasks. There's so much to do and so much to keep track of.

So, how do you track it? Where do you store all this information?

If you don't have your processes documented, it finds a home in your brain, and the problem is that your brain is a precious resource. If you store all your business information in it, you risk overwhelming yourself and affecting your business. Documenting your key processes helps free up brain space and will keep it from overloading.

PAY ATTENTION TO THE SIGNS

In this story, there were a lot of signs.

The CEO is explaining things numerous times, forgetting how they do things, missing important details, and is overall involved in too much. They're reviewing online orders for elements that should be handed off to someone else, which can be made possible by documenting how the process works. They're involving themselves in every single wholesale order, and having to remember how to add a wholesale partner to the system, a clear indication of a missing process. They're missing payments, which could be avoided if they had their vendor invoicing process documented. They're having duplicate meetings with new hires and forgetting to cover key topics, instead of leveraging a documented process.

And the telltale sign, "I can do it faster myself." We've all been there. While you might have to step in sometimes, it should only be seen as a temporary solution. It doesn't help you in the long term.

The more you find yourself in every process and in the weeds, and the more you have to remember how you do each task, the more this should signal to you that you need to document your processes.

THERE'S FREEDOM IN DOCUMENTATION

It might seem daunting to think about documenting your processes. (And let's be real—not so fun. *Quieres hacer cosas más interesantes.*)

But this is exactly the way to give yourself that freedom to do all the fun things in your business. You'll be able to focus on the real needle movers, not feeling like a *loro* that repeats themselves every week. You won't keep all that information in your head and become a bottleneck for your business. Even if it's only an hour or even fifteen minutes, it all adds up. You'll end up spending hours working through tasks instead of freeing up time for important items that'll grow your business.

Especially when you expand, you'll want to create freedom for yourself, and delegate tasks to new people, like bringing in new customers, processing an order, emailing customers, preparing a campaign, ordering inventory, reconciling cash, hiring. Delegation is a superpower, and you'll be best prepared to delegate by having your processes documented.

Plus, documentation happens once. Then you just have to review and make tweaks as changes happen. If you never put in the effort, you risk inefficiently using your time, money, and energy, which can affect your business in a big way.

DOCUMENTATION = PEACE

You can't wear all the hats all the time or for a long time, *amiga*. Week after week of wearing all the hats of strategy, finances, operations, business development, marketing and advertising, IT, etc., will not only lead to brain overload, but will affect you as you move into the next phase of your business.

If all this information lives in your head, you'll have to explain and re-explain it to new people every single time. And the truth is you might not remember exactly how you do things each time. This could lead to inconsistencies in your operations. Your branding. Your customer experience. Your finances. You want the peace of mind that how you and your employees are doing things are aligned with your vision.

Rather than struggling to manage daily tasks and improvising your operations, documenting your processes is the most effective way to ensure consistency. Consistency is calming. It benefits you, your team, and your business because everyone is on the same page. This documentation will show how your business operates—every step, approval, review, and decision point.

THIS DOESN'T JUST APPLY TO TEAMS

Now, you might be thinking this doesn't apply to you because you're a team of "me, myself, and I," currently, but this doesn't just apply to teams. *No te escapas.*

Even if you're a solopreneur for now, it's still putting extra strain on your brain to remember exactly how you do things each time, and like we said earlier, you might not even remember exactly how you do things each time. With this approach, you leave it up to chance. *"Lo hago como me sale."*

So whether you're a solopreneur, a team of five or a team of fifty, documenting your processes is critical to building your beautiful business.

THESE THREE THINGS ARE DIFFERENT

Un pequeño desvío. It's worth mentioning here that "processes" tends to be used in multiple ways that could be confusing. They all have a key part to play in how you set up the documentation of your business, but they have distinct purposes. These are Policies, Processes, and Standard Operating Procedures (the infamous SOPs).

- **Policies** – Policies outline a business's goals, values, and acceptable behaviors. These are documents that speak to principles and give overall guidance.

- **Processes** – Processes provide a big picture look at a set of interrelated tasks. These are documents that show how a process flows from start to finish.

- **Standard Operating Procedures (SOPs)** – SOPs illustrate the detailed view of how a specific task is to be performed. These are documents that walk someone through how to execute.

Now, back to processes.

START SIMPLE WHEN APPLYING IT TO YOUR BUSINESS

This isn't something you want to do all at once. Take a simple approach.

Brainstorm which processes are part of your business operations. List out everything you've worked on for the past few weeks. Be sure to open your calendar to cross-check for anything you might have missed. How many items were related to things that could have been documented? Take a broad sweep initially and then prioritize the processes, separating out some that may be SOPs. Think about which processes are taking up the most brain space, or which processes you plan to delegate soon to an existing or incoming hire.

Taking your top four processes, assign them a documentation timeline over the next six months, or depending on you and your team's capacity.

Keep in mind there are so many ways this can take shape, but as an example, this might look like…

- **Sales** – How do you process orders and deliver products to customers/clients?
- **Inventory** – How is inventory sourced, purchased, and received?
- **Procurement** – How do you select, pay, and receive goods/ services?
- **Finances** – How do you compile, review, and report out on your numbers?

Ultimately you want to have a process map for each key process in your business, but take it at your pace. And do it in a format that works for you, whether that looks like a document (process narrative) or a diagram (process flowchart).

BONUS: TAKE A DEEPER DIVE

Once you hit seven figures, the integrity of your numbers and the processes that feed into them become extremely important to you scaling successfully. This means you'll want to pay special attention to processes that impact your financials, and will want to start to build out a proper internal control environment. Your **internal control environment** is the standards, processes, and structure that provide the basis for ensuring your business is protected from financial inaccuracies, operational inefficiencies, and fraud.

This is a formal structure for protecting your business, to be evolved from your existing process maps. This is achieved by layering in checkpoints and safeguards, also known as internal controls, that'll ensure the integrity of financial and accounting information and keep your business running smoothly.

And the good news is that there's a standard set of processes that one would use when elevating their existing process maps into an internal control environment so you aren't starting from scratch. Typically, you would incorporate approximately ten to twelve key processes: Enterprise (ENT), Financial Accounting and Reporting (FAR), Order to Cash (OTC), Inventory/Source to Supply (S2S), Procure to Pay (P2P), Hire to Retire (H2R), Cash (CASH), Fixed Assets (FA), Leases (LS), Equity (EQ), Taxes (TAX) and Information Technology (IT).

Just like everything else, this should be customized to your business. Naming may vary slightly depending on preference and some processes might not be necessary if not key or not applicable (i.e., you might prefer Hire to Retire be called HR & Payroll, or you may not have any leases in your business).

My employee left me...in the dark.
POV: Accounting Manager

I love a good cafecito in the morning.

That morning I made myself a cortado because I felt like changing it up from my usual black coffee. I was ready to take on the day. I had it all laid out and first up was a meeting with our Accounts Receivable Analyst to discuss outstanding invoices for our wholesale customers. It was something we had been working on getting under control and they had mentioned they had good news for me.

I walked over to the meeting room and they weren't there yet, so I opened my laptop and checked emails in the meantime. As I skimmed new emails, one stood out. My jaw dropped. Subject line: "I'm resigning from my position, effective immediately."

Guess who it was from? Our Accounts Receivable Analyst.

No warning. No transition period. "How could this happen?" I thought. "Who would leave with no notice?" I very quickly realized this day would not go as planned.

*Thoughts filled my head. We hadn't met in a couple weeks, so I had no idea what they were working on, nor did I know how they did things since I was removed from the process. They created the invoices, billed customers, applied payments, and followed up on outstanding invoices. And then the full reality set in: They were the only one in accounts receivable. **My employee left me... in the dark.***

~

AN UNEXPECTED START TO THE DAY

Talk about your day not looking like you thought it would. *¡Qué desgracia!*

This poor Accounting Manager's day and next few weeks were probably a not-so-fun scramble as they worked to reset everything—and the same goes for any employees who were asked to take over the Accounts Receivable Analyst's tasks in the meantime.

Whenever this happens, everyone is affected. Everyone has to shift priorities and work together to understand, recreate, or reverse engineer all the key tasks that the departed employee handled. This might go as deep as what transaction codes they used to add an invoice or apply a payment. This might also involve exposing to customers that your processes weren't in order because you have to reach out to them and figure out the status of certain invoices or payments. This is a mess that you want to avoid—and one that's easily preventable. *¡Evite el dolor de cabeza!*

THERE'S PROTECTION IN DOCUMENTATION

In the previous story, we talked about the freedom and peace that come with documenting your processes. Now we're getting into the protection that comes with it for your business.

It's great to expand your business by hiring employees, but you never want the knowledge of key operations to sit with employees in their head, or in their own files that you don't have access to. Without documenting your processes, you're at high risk of being left in the dark at one point or another because you won't have a complete picture of how your business operates. This makes you vulnerable to whether or not an employee decides to stay, or decides to be kind enough to give you a transition period before leaving. You want to reduce, or eliminate, how an employee departure affects your business.

And a great way to mitigate this risk is by preventing the loss of knowledge from happening in the first place. You want the protection that documenting your processes offers. It's much less painful this way when someone leaves. *El golpe dolerá menos.*

THE PROTECTION GOES FURTHER
THAN A SUDDEN DEPARTURE

We're speaking here about an employee who decides to leave suddenly, but an employee doesn't have to leave to make process documentation valuable. Documenting your processes protects you in so many more ways.

For instance, an employee might need to take a sick day, a medical leave, or time away from work for a family emergency. Another employee might have additional capacity to help out with another task. And maybe another employee just wants to upskill themselves by learning how other tasks are performed.

If you have processes documented, you'll have a much better chance of being able to have someone step in to work on what you need without needing to rely on the other employee to explain it. This protects your business from both unplanned and unwanted idle time.

WHICH EMPLOYEES ARE YOU DEPENDENT ON?

As we've talked about, every business has a unique set of risks and approaches to those risks. It's up to you to determine which risks are applicable to your business, and which you care about enough to take action on.

The specific risk here is over reliance on an employee that has knowledge of a key part of your operations. This is a perfect opportunity to use the SÍARM framework and determine what needs to be done, if anything.

- **Strategize** – Determine if your strategy is to have only one employee know how to execute certain processes or specific tasks. (If all your employees are cross-trained, skip ahead to the next story as this isn't applicable.)

- **Identify** – Identify which processes or specific tasks rely on the one employee who holds the knowledge.

- **Assess** – Assess if the employee's process or specific tasks are key to your operations, and if so, verify that you have it documented. (If they left today, would you be confident that your business could transition tasks quickly, or would it cause an interruption to your operations?)

- **Respond** – Respond based on your assessment. If there's a gap in documentation, take action to document processes.

- **Monitor** – Regroup at a later time to update the exercise, and add any new processes or specific tasks that need to be documented.

Always keep in mind that your risk priorities can change over time, making it important to have continuous risk management in place because you might not have identified anything now, but that could change in a few months as you delegate, hire, or make changes to your operating model.

Three employees doing the same thing—how did that happen?
POV: CEO and Founder

One wholesale partner. Two wholesale partners. Three wholesale partners.

We were expanding and I couldn't be happier. I created a spreadsheet to keep better track of their terms because their contracts were massive, and there was no way I was going to refer back to them each time. I knew the spreadsheet didn't have everything, but I was the one handling wholesale, so it worked just fine.

Eventually, I was able to hire a Wholesale Manager and knew it was time to hand off the reins and let them handle wholesale. I trained them and asked them to create a spreadsheet similar to the one I had. Since mine was mostly chicken scratch, I told them to look at the contracts and create a new one.

I learned this later on, but the Controller had also asked the Accounting Manager to document wholesale partners terms so they would have them easily available for booking accounting entries. Another spreadsheet was created.

I'll also admit that whenever I reviewed anything to do with wholesale, I referred back to my chicken scratch. I didn't even know where the spreadsheet I had asked the Wholesale Manager to prepare was stored. And I definitely didn't know that the accounting department also had one.

*One day we all met to discuss a change in terms for one of our wholesale partners. As we started the meeting, we all pulled out our separate trackers. We laughed. We realized how siloed we were. All in our own worlds documenting the same thing. Oops. **Three employees doing the same thing—how did that happen?***

~

THINGS CAN GET WILD FAST

Having a Wholesale Manager and an accounting team is great. It's exciting to be at the point where your business is increasing in size and complexity. You're no longer taking on all responsibilities. You have a team that you can teach. You have department leads who can teach others too. You no longer have to be the center of everything. All good, right? Maybe.

Because if you're not careful, you could find yourself having multiple employees doing the same thing and not even realizing. Things can become a *locura* very quickly. There's no need for three employees to each be getting paid to track wholesale partner information.

You don't want to risk breeding inefficiencies in your processes, which can leak into the rest of your business and stunt its growth.

DON'T FALL INTO THE TRAP

You might be thinking this could never happen to you, but it's surprisingly easy to get caught up in the day-to-day of your business. You can fall into the trap of believing things seem to be working, "So everything is okay." And while it might be true that things are working, you might be unknowingly introducing inefficiencies into your business, which can multiply over time.

Falling down the "everything is okay" trap also leads to confusion amongst your employees. Whenever you don't have a process laid out, employees will fill in the blanks of what they're responsible for, and how they should do things, which may or may not align with how you envisioned it.

DOCUMENTATION = CLARITY

We've talked about the freedom, peace, and protection that documenting your processes brings in the previous two stories, but now let's talk about how it also brings clarity to how you're running your operations.

By documenting your processes, you allow things to be clear for you, your employees, and your business overall. Everyone is clear on how a process is supposed to flow, on who's doing what, and on key elements within that process when it comes to people involved, important documents used, approval points, systems, etc. You also reduce the risk of silos forming because there's open communication and dialogue between employees as everyone sits together to form and/or align the process document.

And sometimes we really just don't know what we don't know. When you sit and document your processes, you'll know. It'll be clear where you're running duplicate processes because this is absolutely something you want to know sooner than later.

Process mapping will also give you the opportunity to expose where bottlenecks, gaps, or exposures are. You might find out you're in too many processes, you might find a task or approval that's missing, or that something isn't working the way you thought it should be.

Plus, never underestimate the power of having one central document of how a process should work that all employees have access to. Instead of creating several documents that live in different places, you have one file that everyone can use as the main source of record.

It's always better to keep things simple and clear. We need to foster all the efficiencies we can in building our beautiful business.

THINK ABOUT YOUR DUPLICATE PROCESSES

Alright, now it's time to turn inward. Think about where you might have duplicate processes in your business. Are there any processes where it used to be one person but you've since expanded? Are there any processes that involve multiple groups where there might be synergies to explore—for instance, with wholesale and accounting like in this example, or sourcing and legal? Where might there be documents that can be shared as opposed to everyone having their own?

Chapter 8

Every Process Warrants Careful Design: Inefficient Operations Can Cost You Time, Money, and Energy

A fter you've realized the power of documenting your processes, it's time to dig deeper into each specific process so you don't cost yourself time, money, and energy, or expose yourself to negative consequences. Whether it's how you set up your processes around suppliers, partnerships, customers, fulfillment, returns or payroll, the more you carefully design each process, the more you'll generate immense value for your business. In this chapter, we'll walk through how to think about risks as you design each of your processes so that you can create efficient and effective operations across your business.

I relied on one supplier and it blew up in my face.
POV: VP of Supply Chain

Our new collection was amazing.

I was proud of the entire collection, but my absolute favorite piece was a dress that paid tribute to the rich, vibrant colors of Latin American cultures. It was the hero piece of the collection. We had carefully selected all the fabrics, buttons, and threads, pouring through hundreds of samples to get it just right. The months of talking to suppliers to make sure they understood exactly what we needed had come to fruition.

Now all that was left was to finalize the orders so we could make the items and get them to market for all to enjoy. Our suppliers confirmed that all materials would be sent out that week and would be delivered in the next month.

One by one, we got everything in to start building the piece—except for the buttons. We followed up and followed up again. We called and called again. Finally, we couldn't wait any longer or we would miss our target launch dates. We rushed to find a new supplier.

We found one just in time. It would be for a new button that would work, but unfortunately wasn't quite the original vision. Once we found a backup, we had to pay the rush fees too. That was a lesson I could have done without. ***I relied on one supplier and it blew up in my face.***

~

THEY DISAPPEARED

Where did their supplier go? They decided it was better to become a ghost than to respond. *Desapareció como un fantasma.*

This could happen to anyone. Even if you've spent months working with someone and talking through logistics of how everything will go, you just never know. *Porque uno nunca sabe.*

Fortunately, they were able to recover, but the reality might not always look like this. They could easily have been left stranded, launching the collection without its hero piece.

RELYING ON ONE SUPPLIER CAN COST YOU

Any time you rely on a supplier, you're putting yourself at risk. Yes, you may have a long-standing relationship with them. Yes, they might deliver a great ingredient, a great material, a great product or great packaging. They may not have let you down up to this point. But it's possible for them to fail you at one point or another, whether intentionally or due to circumstances outside of their control. And that means a risk to you if you can't carry on as planned.

You want to have top of mind which supplier relationships are single source, meaning they're your one and only source of that specific product or service. Basically, if they would have a severe impact (basically halt) your operations if they stop working with you, go out of business, or stop carrying what you source from them, then they should be deemed high risk.

You want to be aware of where you have these dependencies so you can *consciously* make decisions to accept the risk, or take actions to mitigate the risk. In other words, it doesn't mean you will or won't take the risk on—it just means that you're proceeding with eyes wide open to the risks you could face. *Con ojos abiertos.*

THIS PRINCIPLE GOES BEYOND SUPPLIERS

While this story is focused on suppliers that support your product (i.e., direct vendors), the same goes for vendors that help support your operations (i.e., indirect vendors). These are all other vendors that provide products or services—warehouse space, electricity, internet, furniture, office supplies, PR services, legal services, subscriptions, etc.

Putting your trust in one vendor can also mean a risk to your business if not managed properly.

And taking it further, single-source dependencies exist on the other side too. Whenever you rely on a few customers or clients to bring in the majority of your revenue, you're also taking on risk. You don't know if customers will keep purchasing your product, or if clients will renew your contract. Many businesses have been left scrambling to recover when a retailer decides to stop carrying their product in store, or if a large client decides not to renew their contract. For those of us with businesses that are getting off the ground and face additional hurdles just to stay in business, the sudden loss of cash flow could be detrimental.

BE PROACTIVE INSTEAD

A lot of risk management comes down to being proactive. *Por si las moscas.*

It's about how you anticipate what could happen, and what you do with that information. Of course you hope you don't need to deal with negative events, but you might, and that's where identifying your risks helps you grow your business into a beautiful one, one that's protected and resilient because it's ready for anything that comes its way. Sometimes having a backup plan is half the battle!

Now, practically speaking, this doesn't mean you have to identify a backup for every single supplier, vendor, or customer that you have—that would be impossible. What you want to do is spend your energy efficiently, by prioritizing those with the highest risk profile, meaning those that'll affect your business the most. For instance, it's not that big of a deal if a popular office supplies chain goes out of business as there are plenty of other stores that have office supplies.

ASSESS YOUR SINGLE-SOURCE DEPENDENCY RISK

So, when it comes to your business—how well prepared are you? Let's do a single-source risk assessment for your business.

- **Suppliers** – Who are your suppliers? Depending on what type of business you have, think about ingredients, materials, products and/or packaging. For each item, identify the primary supplier and a backup. If you don't have a backup supplier, make a plan to find one, or identify how you would pivot if something goes wrong with that supplier.

- **Vendors** – Who are your vendors? Pull your last year of expenses and look for vendors and what you spend on each. Filter top to bottom based on where you spend the most to give you an additional viewpoint. Before going through the full exercise of assigning backups, go through the list and disregard any vendors that correspond to categories that you identify as low risk (e.g., office supplies). Once you have your list of vendors that are medium to high risk, identify the primary supplier and a backup. If you don't have a backup vendor, make a plan to find one, or identify how you would pivot if something goes wrong with that vendor.

- **Customers** – Who are your customers? Do you have a customer, or a few customers, that you're relying on for 80% or more of your business? This one isn't necessarily about finding a backup customer, but about being aware of it and knowing that if this is how your business runs, you should proactively think of ways to protect yourself. Maybe you diversify revenue streams. Maybe you think about how to have the client commit to up-front payments or a longer renewal period. Maybe you make a shift to increase your business savings so you can mitigate the loss of cash flow.

With these exercises, you'll be in the best position to be aware of what's happening in your business. And when faced with adversity, you'll be able to pivot and bounce back much more quickly.

BONUS: TAKE A DEEPER DIVE

If you're a product-based business and store all your inventory in one location, this is also a single-source dependency! And one that's very important to pay attention to.

Consider building out a formal business continuity plan, which is a document that outlines all critical information so that your business can continue operating should an unplanned incident occur (e.g., top SKUs, key systems, warehouse map, contact information, etc.). It identifies everything from who to contact and how to respond so that operations can be minimally interrupted. It also includes a disaster recovery plan that specifically focuses on the IT systems and infrastructure that'll enable you, as the name implies, to recover from a disaster.

I recommend starting with a scenario planning exercise where you brainstorm everything that could go wrong and how you would respond. Fires, earthquakes, system outages, blackouts, strikes— anything that would interfere with you accessing your inventory or getting orders out. Once you have that, document what your business would do in each of these scenarios, everything from the person responsible, the steps to take and the timeline to follow is helpful so that when it happens, you can take action.

The goal is for you to feel safe and secure that your business is prepared and can rebound quickly when the unexpected happens.

(And then longer term when you have the capacity and the funds, you can add multiple warehouses to mitigate the overall single-source dependency risk.)

I left myself exposed with this partnership agreement.

POV: Senior Manager of Partnerships

We finally landed a dream partnership!

We had been working on it for months and we finally closed the deal. They were a great company that would definitely elevate our brand and give us an opportunity to boost sales through a signature collection we would create together. The partnership was to be structured primarily as a royalty with us paying them $1.50 per product we sold. As part of the agreement, we also agreed that the royalty paid to them would be reduced by any physical returns of the product. It seemed simple enough and we signed on the dotted line.

Moving forward, our Partnerships Manager was in charge of the process. Reports were pulled. Royalties were calculated. Payments were made.

This went on for several months.

Once it came time to renew the contract, our VP of Supply Chain happened to be in a meeting where we were discussing returns, and we were surprised to learn that we weren't receiving physical returns at the warehouse. Oh no. That meant that the royalty check we sent to our partner was inaccurate—because how could we reduce the check amount by physical returns if we didn't receive them?

It turned out we had been using refund data instead of physical returns data to reduce royalties due to our partner—meaning our calculation was incorrect all these months. We were underpaying them.

This prompted us to do a full contract review, where we discovered another inaccuracy. The royalty calculation also didn't include any partnership product where it was included in a bundle because we hadn't even thought about that scenario in the contract negotiations.

We couldn't leave it like this. We redid the royalty calculation and payment, and issued an additional check to them for the missing royalties. The relationship continued, but the truth remained. **I left myself exposed with this partnership agreement.**

~

IT'S NOT ALWAYS WHAT'S ON THE SURFACE

Surface level, one might say it's the Partnership Manager's fault. They should have done more research on what they were pulling and brought it to someone's attention. But they weren't the ones who had negotiated the contract.

It extends further than one manager who didn't realize their mistake. *No les culpes.*

While both parties entered into the agreement in good faith with terms that were seemingly clear, in this case, the royalty could never be paid according to the terms stated. The royalty calculation was always going to be inaccurate. (I mean—how can physical returns be a factor in the calculation when no physical returns are coming to the warehouse? It's physically impossible.) And not only that, the calculation was always going to be incomplete because bundles were overlooked.

By signing an agreement with terms that you can't comply with, you risk putting yourself in jeopardy from both a legal and reputational perspective, not to mention from an accounting perspective because your numbers are also recorded incorrectly. There are multiple layers here and I don't want this to happen to you.

ROOT CAUSE ANALYSIS TOOL TO THE RESCUE

So, what caused this, and how do we prevent it from happening in the future? This type of scenario is a perfect opportunity for a **root cause analysis**, which is one of my favorite tools to use when something goes wrong. Because things will go wrong. It's inevitable. But it's how we recover from it that'll set us up for success. *Somos resilientes.*

Essentially, we ask why, and why again, and again. Typically, somewhere between three and five why's should get you to the root cause that'll allow you to find the right solution.

- Why did this happen? Well, the Partnership Manager should have known what they were doing.

- Asking why again, there should have been further communication with relevant departments to understand what reports were being pulled and if the reports were accurate (e.g., sales, inventory, and customer service departments).

- Asking why again, there should have been more due diligence up-front before the contract was even signed to verify the reports existed and could be pulled accurately.

- Asking why again, this goes beyond this particular partnership agreement. There should be a process in place to ensure any reports listed in an agreement are vetted up-front with all parties involved before entering into the agreement.

PREVENT THE SITUATION MOVING FORWARD

¡Y listo! With this information, you know that the best solution to prevent this from happening again is to update the contract process. You know that there needs to be a better process in place to vet agreements, and any data or reports that are required as part of it.

By doing it this way, you're implementing a solution that'll have a much larger impact on your business. You're mitigating your risk by preventing this situation from occurring not just in partnership agreements, but in all agreements entered into by your business. Now you'll find out before signing the contract what you can or cannot provide.

You might find that the report can't be provided as stated or at all. You might find that the report requires too much manual manipulation and it's not worth the time or energy to create it. You'll also have the opportunity to think through all scenarios that may happen; for instance, if the product will or will not be included with other products and how those will be handled (e.g., the bundles).

AGREE TO TERMS THAT WORK FOR YOU

In this story, after their correction and apology tour, they'll want to adjust the terms to ones that work for them so that it's something they can provide accurately, and simply.

If they don't accept physical returns, and don't plan to update that anytime soon, they should consider negotiating terms so the agreement is in line with something they can comply with; for example, they could agree to reduce the royalties by a flat percentage of historical returns (i.e., 3%). Doing it this way is helpful because it no longer requires spending time pulling reports and calculating exact amounts every single month. Instead, the calculation becomes simple math based on a reasonable return rate that both parties agree to, one that only has to be revisited when the contract is renewed. This would make everyone's life easier and eliminate the risk of noncompliance.

CONTRACTS PROTECT BOTH PARTIES

Now you've seen the multiple layers of risk that are hidden in the contract onion. If we don't peel them back and take the time to understand them, *nos va a hacer llorar la cebolla jaja.*

Whether it's for a product, service, project, independent contractor, influencer, affiliate, speaker, event, etc., contracts help protect you by laying out the key terms of the arrangement you're entering into. This way you keep expectations clear between you and the other party.

Anytime you don't have a signed contract, you're accepting the risk of not having it in place. (The only circumstance where this might be okay is if you've done your risk assessment, and this is the response you're comfortable with based on your risk appetite. Don't tell your lawyer friends.)

HOW DO YOU ENTER INTO CONTRACTS?

Take some time to assess your contract process. Taking the first layer, what types of arrangements do you enter into? Do you have contracts for none, some, or all of them? Do you have a set criterion for which types of arrangements require a contract, and are there some you're okay with taking a risk on?

Taking the next layer, who's involved in the process? Do you have lawyer-drafted templates that you use? Do you have a lawyer on retainer or in-house that assists you in drafting and reviewing contracts? Do you involve other relevant parties when appropriate (e.g., wholesale, IT, supply chain, etc.)?

Taking another layer, are you confident that all the terms you have in your agreements make sense? Does it include all scenarios? Can you deliver what you're committing to? If you aren't sure, this is an ideal time to review your contracts to verify that you can.

While this may seem like a lot of work, discussion, planning, and vetting up-front, it'll prevent headaches down the line. You want to become friends with risk by knowing your contract process, how you negotiate contract terms, and how you'll execute them.

BONUS: TAKE A DEEPER DIVE

The more you can solidify your contract process with your team, the less you have to remember and less hands-on you have to be to make sure everything goes right. The process will take care of itself. When you're ready and/or have the capital, implement a manual checklist, or invest in a contract management system, to make sure all contracts are going through a consistent process.

Our chaotic approach to customer orders was hurting us.

POV: Director of Wholesale

I got in my car and drove to work, blasting Selena to get me ready for the day ahead.

The closer I got, the more this feeling of dread sunk in. It was nearing the end of the month and I could feel the ticking of the clock. The accounting team was breathing down my neck to get everything updated so they could close this month's books.

I had so many orders to get through. I knew I would be sitting there reviewing each open order line by line, and updating every order in the system with its current status, whether it was a new order being placed, an order that was now shipped, or an order that needed to be billed.

The amount of work I had to do every month was out of control because of all the ways new orders came in. Some were placed through EDI. Some via a customer's portal. Some via email. In all cases, pricing wasn't automated, which was the most important factor because we had to make sure they were paying us the right amount. Since the customer could input their own pricing, we always had to double-check it was right. And by we, I mean me, because I knew each customer's details from memory, so I would review every single order. Every day, every month. Every single SKU number, quantity, pricing, discount, line by line.

I would do the same with orders that were now shipped. For that, I had to verify in multiple systems whether orders had been shipped because our systems didn't talk to each other.

And the same with billing. Even though at least for that I had help from the Accounts Receivable Analyst, thank goodness, though they were also burdened with meticulously reviewing each line item to avoid any corrections and complaints from customers later on.

Safe to say—this was not the most efficient way to handle this process every month, but I couldn't rely on the system or any automations to help me with orders. Instead, I kept a manual spreadsheet to monitor exactly where

every order was in the process. I knew this wasn't going to work much longer.
Our chaotic approach to customer orders was hurting us.

~

IMPERFECT ACTION IS GREAT, INITIALLY

When you start a business, it's okay, and expected that you take imperfect action and get scrappy. You're trying to get it up and running as best you can. You say yes to opportunities that'll bring in sales. *¡Necesitamos los centavitos!*

You might be excited to bring in one customer. Two. Three. You see the growth in your business, and you keep making it work with a *como se pueda* approach. But imagine if you had a seven-figure business with thirty-six customers and hundreds of orders, and your Director of Wholesale manually reviews every single order, line by line. *Uyyy no.*

WORKAROUNDS AND BAND-AIDS ONLY GO SO FAR

While the wholesale team in this story may be able to absorb a process like this one in the short term, in the long term, they won't be able to sustain it without better solutions. This process will continue to become more and more cumbersome as additional customers are added.

If this were you:

Yes, in the short term, you can have the team remember all the different steps to process a customer order and the nuances of each one, but in the long term, you'll force them to spend all their time doing manual, tedious tasks versus focusing on value-add endeavors.

Yes, in the short term, you can hire and bring in more heads to process customer orders, but in the long term, you're really just throwing people at the problem versus fixing the problem.

Not to mention that anytime you have manual intervention in any transaction, you introduce a higher likelihood of human error. And if you have too many errors, this could affect your relationship with your customers, and could affect your finances if you're billing for orders incorrectly.

So yes, there are temporary solutions, but we're out here trying to build beautiful businesses that maximize impact. We can't do it if we implement practices that are merely getting us by.

GETTING TO THE NEXT LEVEL

Once you have several customers, you want to think about how you can update your processes to match where you are now. You want to understand where you have introduced unnecessary complexities, and make a plan of action to pivot before they compound on each other. Otherwise, you risk making the process so cumbersome that you hinder your ability to grow and scale.

If you think about it now, how many customers are you working with? How do you onboard them? How many distinct variations would you have on how you receive orders, how you input pricing, how you send inventory, how you issue invoices, how you confirm receipt of goods, or how you process credits or refunds? How many points of human error are you exposing yourself to?

MAP OUT YOUR CUSTOMER PROCESS

Create a process map of how your customers place orders. Once you have it mapped out, spend time assessing the process and identifying where you have added complexities. For each pain point, put a plan of action in place to reduce the complexity so you can streamline the process and mitigate the risk going forward.

- **If you're early on in your journey, you're in luck.** You can understand your current process through your process map, and design a customer onboarding process that works for you. As you automate, you can plan accordingly to have all customers follow a similar process (or as much as possible, because some nuances are expected).

- **If you already have several customers, you have a bit more work to do, but it'll be worth it long term.** You'll want to take the process map that you created and identify where the largest variations are. Then identify what the solution would be. Is it streamlining the process? Is it creating a new interface? Is it changing your contract? And how long will it take? Work with your technology team to understand and prioritize changes that need to be made.

This exercise will also highlight where your wholesale team is spending their time. Do you think they're spending their time efficiently, or are there shifts to be made? You might realize that you're putting pressure on your wholesale team and making these changes will help them shift to value-add activities that'll keep them happier and your business growing.

THINK THIS SCENARIO DOESN'T APPLY TO YOU?

Some of you might be reading this and thinking this is just some fun *chisme* because this doesn't apply to you. But I want you to think about applying the overall takeaway, which is that you want to avoid introducing unnecessary complexities in your business that could prevent you from getting to the next level.

So, think about your business beyond the scenario illustrated in this story. Where have you used more of a workaround approach? Where do you feel like you have complexities that could be unraveled to make the process more efficient? For instance, it could be your client process, your inventory process, your podcast process, your social media process—any process that you need to better understand where you stand so you can put yourself in the best position to scale. Once you've selected a process, go through the exercise of mapping it out and identifying where and how you can improve it.

The wrong invoice went into the customer's package.
POV: Fulfillment Manager

We had a big day ahead of filling online orders.

We grabbed all the essentials. Boxes—check. Shipping material—check. Tape—check. Inserts—check. We selected the orders we were ready to fulfill. We did thirty at a time because that felt like a manageable amount. We printed out the shipping labels and the invoices that would go in each box.

It was always fun to see what people ordered. Some orders were small—one mascara or one foundation. Others were larger—one eye shadow, one brush, and one foundation. We even had one huge one that must have been an order from a makeup artist that was stocking up—ten eye shadow pallets, five foundations, and a ton of brushes. Every item was carefully placed into its respective box.

It was nearing 1 p.m., so we paused for lunch, leaving the products inside their boxes and the invoices sitting outside with the marketing inserts. After enjoying some delicious tacos al pastor, we made our way back to the office to finish the orders.

By the end of the day, the packages were on the way to our customers.

A few days later, an email was sent to our support team saying that their order had been received with the incorrect invoice inside. The customer was concerned that they had someone else's name and address, which likely meant someone else had theirs. We apologized profusely. **The wrong invoice went into the customer's package.**

~

NOT EVERY CUSTOMER IS FORGIVING

While the customer was forgiving in this situation and recommended the business verify how this happened to prevent it in the future, this could have just as easily been a customer who was furious that their data was out there. They could have written a bad review, reported it, and never purchased the product again.

Instead of delivering the seamless customer experience that I'm sure you envision for your product, this situation could put your ratings and your reputation at risk. Plus, if they had been a bad actor themselves, they could have used the name, address, and phone number of the person whose invoice they received for malicious intent.

SMALL MISTAKES CAN SNOWBALL

Seemingly small mistakes can snowball into huge threats to your business if not addressed promptly. This is why when something goes wrong, you immediately want to understand why it went wrong so you can resolve it moving forward. *No queremos que pase otra vez.*

Hopefully you're already thinking this, but this is a great time to leverage the root cause analysis tool (first discussed in the partnership agreement story).

It may be the case that it was:

- An isolated incident due to human error, in which case you can pass on making an update as long as the process is designed well.

- A lack of training, in which case all employees who handle shipping should be retrained and acknowledge they understand the proper process.

- A gap in process, in which case the process should be updated; for instance, maybe all orders could be completely packaged without a gap (e.g., lunch) so the opportunity for invoices to move around before packages are closed is reduced.

- Or maybe there needs to be an additional verification during the process, in which case the process should be enhanced; for instance, all packages could be double-checked by a second person to verify the name on the invoice matches the name on the shipping label.

These are just a few examples of what the root cause could be and how you can address it. Remember that each situation is unique and will require a remediation that fits your business.

IT CAN'T BE EMPHASIZED ENOUGH

Speaking of customer information, I can't emphasize enough the importance of handling personal, sensitive, or confidential data with care. Customer names, home addresses, email addresses, and birthdays should be protected and should only be available to those who need it.

Also, you should have explicit permission to share a customer's name or testimonial as it can be linked back to them. (Yes, I know we all get excited to share our customer's order that we just packed, or that they just purchased one of your service offerings, *pero ojo*, because you could be putting yourself at risk.)

Privacy even applies internally. For instance, if you have a team communication platform with open channels, including one in which your support team communicates regarding customers' orders (using their names, addresses, and emails), this means that all your employees can access this information. But since not all your employees need it, this should be in a private channel that only those who need it can access.

THIS APPLIES TO OTHER TYPES OF INFORMATION TOO

In addition to customer information, data privacy extends to vendor and employee information as well. It's all considered personal identifiable information (PII) that needs to be protected by any business that's processing or in possession of an individual's sensitive information.

Basically, PII includes any data that when pieced together with another piece of data can give you the identity of the person. So you might think that by having first names in your file, you're okay, but if you also have a city, or maybe a birthday, someone could figure out the identity of the person. It's considered PII and must be safeguarded. *Nadie quiere estar expuesto.*

The risk here is that you accidentally reveal PII that could lead to legal implications and fines, or distrust from customers when it comes to how you're managing their personal data. Become friends with risk by knowing how you're managing and protecting data in your business.

WHICH PROCESSES HOLD SENSITIVE INFORMATION IN YOUR BUSINESS?

Where do you have the most sensitive information in your customer, vendor, and employee processes? Identify the areas, assess the risk, and respond accordingly so you can ensure you have proper data protection.

I'd also recommend training your employees on what PII is, how to prevent revealing it, and what to do if they identify instances of it being revealed. This will go a long way in protecting your beautiful business.

It was costing too much to require returns be sent back—who knew?
POV: Director of Operations

We had decided early on that great customer service would be our top priority.

We wanted our customers to be happy and to keep coming back for more. If they weren't happy, we would always make it right. If their product wasn't the right color, style, fit, or they had just changed their mind, we would issue a refund, no questions asked. We would even cover the return shipping cost to bring the product back to our warehouse. We wanted to make it a no-brainer for them to purchase from us, and keep purchasing from us.

This worked well for a while. But over time, we saw shipping costs increasing more and more, to levels we hadn't seen before. I remember one P&L meeting thinking, "Enough is enough. We have to figure this out." So I asked our Operations Manager to look into these costs.

They came back to me a couple days later with their findings. And while yes, shipping costs were rising overall, which we expected, there were return shipping costs bulked in the same account. I asked them to pull out those costs into their own P&L line so we could compare apples to apples. I also asked them to dig further into the returns process overall because I felt like there was more going on there.

Well, they understood the assignment—and I'm so glad they did.

A couple weeks later, we had all the information on the returns process. There definitely was more going on there beyond shipping costs. It was costing us money and time across multiple teams to process returns—customer service, warehouse, and accounting, and it was costing us to store the returned products that weren't even going to be resold. Between the costs and the time we were asking our employees to spend on the returns process, it was too much.

We sat down and analyzed if it was worth it to require the product be sent back to us. Our final answer: no. Not only was it costing us more to bring the product back, but it was taking up too much time to process returns.

We made a plan to stop asking for the product back, which freed up money and time. And the best part is that it was still in line with our strategy because customers were even happier to not go through the hassle of returning the product. **It was costing too much to require returns be sent back—who knew?**

~

BECAUSE WE THINK WE SHOULD

It's often the case that we set up processes a certain way because we see others doing it. For product-based businesses, most have a returns process. Most want the item back if the customer is requesting a refund. It's what we think we should do.

But what we miss with this approach is doing our own analysis on what works for our business. In this story, you can see how easy it is sometimes to overlook something until something is staring you in the face (e.g., shipping costs) and it prompts you to look into it. Thankfully they were able to course correct, but it's not uncommon for businesses to have tunnel vision when it comes to setting up processes, and to let them continue inefficiently until there's a big issue.

THE BIGGER PICTURE

If we don't zoom out, we miss the bigger picture when it comes to our processes, and how we're operating our business. We miss being able to view things from a better vantage point, which provides much clearer insights into how we should be using our resources.

With an integrated analysis, we're able to see all the time, money, and energy that go into a process. We're able to see how this affects our finances. We're able to see who's involved. We're able to ask ourselves if it aligns with our strategy and our values. It's important to take a step back and consider all the factors.

Plus, by involving others, we're also inviting those who're affected by the process to weigh in and point out other factors we may be missing. Especially with something like the returns process, there are so many teams involved—strategy, operations, customer service, accounting, to name a few.

THERE ARE MANY FACTORS TO CONSIDER

Pretend you're in their shoes and you're conducting your own integrated analysis on the returns process. You've involved all the key players, collected all the relevant data, and come up with your findings.

These may be some of them:

- You might have found that the cost of shipping is higher than the cost to make the original product. (And even if you can resell, it doesn't make up for it.)

- You might have found that your customer service team spends an additional five minutes on the phone with each customer to process a return (e.g., to get shipping details and issue the label). This is five minutes that quickly multiplies and takes away from other focuses. And if you're paying a third party to help, there's likely a specific cost by type of transaction.

- You might have found that your warehouse team spends a few hours receiving, processing and logging the return (maybe even manually), which detracts from them receiving and working with new inventory and comes with cost as well.

- You might have found that your accounting team spends additional time estimating and adjusting for returned inventory.

- You might also have found that your returns process doesn't have all the necessary SOPs, so to continue this process, you would need to spend time creating these.

When all is said and done, the analysis reveals that the money, time, and energy that goes into running a returns process that requires the product be sent back by a customer isn't the best for your business. Your resources can be better spent elsewhere.

THERE MIGHT BE OTHER BENEFITS TOO

You might also find that from a strategic perspective, a solution like this adds value to your brand and customer experience because the returns process becomes a hassle-free experience.

And by offering a meaningful alternative, you create additional goodwill that keeps customers coming back. You might ask them to donate the product to a local organization if you're community driven. Or you might explain how they can dispose of it to reduce the carbon emissions that it would take to send the product back if you're sustainability-driven. (They might even write you amazing reviews for innovative approaches like this.)

BAD ACTORS EXIST EVERYWHERE

And before you come after me—yes, there are bad actors that may take advantage of not having to return a product. There are and they might. *Siempre habrá quienes se aprovechen. Los malagradecidos.*

But the reality is that the vast majority of people are good people and they won't.

Have you benefited from a generous return policy? Have you taken malicious advantage of it? (I know of a great pet brand that has outstanding customer service and doesn't require the product to be returned and I've never taken advantage of this. I simply keep coming back because I know I'm in good hands.)

The great news is that with a risk lens, you can also put detective checkpoints in place that keep an eye on any red flags.

For instance, you could determine a healthy refund rate for your business—let's say 5%—and if returns go above this rate, you investigate further. You could also implement an automated flagging system at the customer service level where customers get flagged for excessively requesting refunds—let's say maybe 4x per year. And you could even design the process where any refunds on orders above a certain amount—let's say $500—the merchandise has to be returned. This way you prevent any excessive abuse when you remove your returns process.

The beauty of this is that you can architect it the way that you want to based on your risk appetite.

DO AN INTEGRATED ANALYSIS ON ONE OF YOUR PROCESSES

The easiest way to identify one of your processes that may benefit from an integrated analysis is by looking at your finances because it's the first place you'll see red flags.

The next time you review your finances, whether it's on your own, with your CFO, or at your next P&L meeting, pay attention to significant cost drivers. Maybe it's a product or ingredient costing way more than usual. Maybe it's warehouse rent that has gone up outside of a normal range. Maybe it's travel expenses that seem too high. Once you've done that, identify what specific process the underlying reason for the cost corresponds to, and ask yourself if there may be something deeper there to unravel. If the answer is yes, take a similar approach to what we walked through.

Here is a checklist of important factors to consider as you execute an **integrated analysis** over a process to ultimately determine whether it should continue:

- **Teams** – Who's involved and who does this affect? (Don't leave employees out of the loop who have a stake in it and could bring valuable input.)

- **Cost** – List out all expenses incurred for this process or specific task.

- **Time** – List out all hours spent on this process or specific task. (Translate it to cost too, if possible.)

- **Strategy** – Understand how well this aligns with your strategy and values.

- **Customers** – If applicable, what impact does this process or specific task have on the customer? Is there an alternative approach they would prefer/benefit from?

A word of caution: this isn't meant to prompt you to go overboard analyzing all your processes to death. *No te pases.* It's simply meant to help you think through how you can better analyze your processes to consider all the factors. This is what will enable you to make informed decisions that'll help your business grow and scale.

And finally, remember that any yes is a no to something else. Any process or task you give your team is a no to something else they could be working on.

My employee's retirement savings were affected because of me.

POV: Employee Benefits Manager

I was honored to have been chosen for the challenge.

Things had been going really well in my role and I was excited to lead the system implementation for our new retirement platform. It was a much-needed update. Our prior system was outdated, and it fell short of the user experience that we wanted for our employees.

For the most part, it was a lift and shift, meaning we wanted the system to serve the same purpose, hold the same information, and execute the same actions. An employee would make their retirement elections and select their percentages, and then the amount would automatically be deducted from their paycheck every pay period. And if they made any changes, the system would automatically update it in the next pay cycle. Pretty simple.

We rolled it out in record time.

Months went by and everything seemed to be going well, until one afternoon I received an email from an employee who had noticed a discrepancy.

They had reviewed their recent paycheck and noticed that there were no retirement deductions in that paycheck. Or the one before that. Or in any of their paychecks going back six months—which was when they last made a change to their percentage.

They went on to say that they also checked the system to make sure it wasn't their error, and maybe they had forgotten to hit Submit, but their election in the retirement system was correct.

"Hmm," I thought. Something wasn't working correctly. Something must have gone wrong in the interface between the retirement system and the payroll system. I apologized, and we updated their election manually.

Unfortunately for them though, the thousands that should have been deposited into their retirement account weren't there—that and the compounding effect of how those contributions would have grown over those six months. **My employee's retirement savings were affected because of me.**

~

IT'S NOT THE EMPLOYEE'S FAULT

¡Pues es su culpa! It might be easy to blame the employee here. They should be reviewing their paycheck. They should make sure their *centavitos* are going where they should be.

But the ownership here is on you as the employer because the employee shouldn't have the responsibility to make sure your systems are working. They're relying on you to implement systems that work the way they should.

Plus, you want the employee to be dedicated to carrying out the responsibilities for their own role in your business. If you had fifteen employees verifying their paycheck each period, that's brain space they could be using elsewhere to help you grow your business. (See the first story in chapter 7 if you need a refresher on the importance of brain space.)

LET'S TALK ABOUT INTERNAL CONTROLS

This is a perfect time to talk more in depth about internal controls and what they are. It's not as complicated as it sounds. *No te me escondas jaja.*

Internal controls, or controls for short, are checkpoints and safeguards that keep your business protected and running smoothly. They maintain the integrity of your business, specifically helping you ensure your financial and accounting information is complete, accurate, and timely. They help you mitigate risks!

These controls can be either manual or automated controls, and we'll get more into this shortly. (And sometimes you'll have manual controls with an automated component.)

Especially when dealing with a system as we are in this story, you would think that once the system is implemented it would run itself. You set up the interface between the retirement system and the payroll system, and you expect any changes to interface accurately each time. But things don't always happen as expected, and that's why you want to be prepared.

YOU CAN IMPLEMENT AN AUTOMATED CONTROL

With interfaces, the biggest risk is that the interface isn't working—so you want an automated control that signals you as to whether or not your systems are communicating effectively.

For example, the automated control here could be in the form of an error report that automatically comes to you, or whoever you designate, if anything with the interface process goes wrong.

It would indicate if the interface didn't execute properly, or it would highlight any specific items that didn't transmit properly. It could be received on a daily, weekly, and/or monthly basis, depending how often the interface runs. Ideally it's blank because there are no errors, but sometimes it'll have some, and that's what will prompt you to investigate. With it, you can have confidence that the interface is working and, in this case, that your employees are getting their retirement funds.

Especially with system implementations, it's really easy to forget to move over all the parts that existed in the previous system like the interface error report control. But a beautiful business doesn't leave its risk lens behind when implementing new systems. (Hopefully by the end of this book, you'll bring your risk lens with you everywhere!)

YOU CAN IMPLEMENT A MANUAL CONTROL

You can even go further to implement a manual control, or two, or three. This gives you additional comfort that the system is doing what it needs to do. There are several ways to do this depending on your resources, capacity, and risk appetite.

For instance, this could look like a reasonableness review. This is where you estimate what the retirement deductions should be for that month (i.e., 8% of salary) and if the amount deducted is within your expected range, you deem it reasonable. But if anything significant pops up, you investigate.

It could also look like a validation review. This is where you select a handful of employees and validate that their retirement deductions from their paycheck are accurate by recalculating what it should be and comparing it to what was deducted. Depending on how big your team is, the selection criteria could be a number or a percentage (e.g., five employees or 10% of all employees).

And finally, if you have no appetite for error, or if you don't have confidence in the interface, you can perform a full check of every single employee. (This is extreme, but could be warranted in certain situations.)

WHAT SYSTEMS DO YOU HAVE IN YOUR BUSINESS?

You need systems to help you start, grow, and scale your business—there's no way around it. Even if it's just a few systems, or hundreds of systems, knowing how well your systems are working is extremely important in building a beautiful business. And the best way to become friends with systems risk is by knowing what systems you have, how your systems work within your processes, and paying special attention to any system implementations.

Make a list of all the systems you use in your business. Are you comfortable that your systems are working correctly? If there are interfaces, how do you know that they're interfacing correctly? Are there any automated or manual controls you're curious to implement in your business?

BONUS: TAKE A DEEPER DIVE

As you scale, your tech stack is bound to evolve, and before they become unmanageable, I highly recommend keeping a centralized list of your systems. This doesn't have to be a very comprehensive or complicated list. It's more to keep track of your technology ecosystem: what systems you have, why you use them, and how critical they are to your business's operations and financials.

Having this consolidated view will keep you prepared and protected in the case of disasters or changes that affect your operations because you'll know which ones to focus on. And checking this periodically will also help you understand where you may have a duplicate system, where you may be spending money where you shouldn't, or where employees may have implemented systems that don't align or weren't approved. It's a win-win-win.

Chapter 9

Protect Yourself from Fraud: Overlooking Gaps in Your Processes Can Make You Vulnerable to Bad Actors

The dreaded word: fraud. The reality is that at one point or another most businesses are subject to fraud, and the perpetrators can work from the inside or outside to commit it. It could be an impersonator who pretends to be a vendor, it could be a cybercriminal who poses as you, or beloved employees who betray your trust. Either way, it's crucial you plug any gaps where bad actors can infiltrate your business. In this chapter, we'll discuss how to incorporate fraud risk considerations into your processes so you can proactively keep your business safe.

We sent money to the wrong bank account.
POV: Controller

I'll never forget the look of sheer panic on their face.

Let me back up.

That morning, like every Thursday morning, I approved invoices for payment. This batch included all invoices that were due that week. After my review, everything looked good, and I approved all the invoices in the system. Check.

I moved on to the next few to-dos on my list. Check. Check.

My 11 a.m. meeting was to discuss an accounting entry for inventory that we needed to make as part of our month-end close. I settled into the conference room, turned on the main screen to see our virtual attendees, and we shared what we planned to have for lunch. As we were about to start, our Accounting Manager burst into the room. They asked if I had already approved invoices that morning. The look on their face when I nodded and said yes. I could tell we had a problem.

I quickly walked out of the room with them. They explained that there was a problem with a couple of our invoices. One of our vendors had changed their bank account twice within the last two months, and while the first change was legitimate, the second one was not.

We hoped we could do something and we definitely tried to, but it was too late. The payments were already initiated and on their way to who knows what bank account, and there was no way to stop it. We had fallen victim to cybercriminals. We sent $38,000 to a bank account that didn't belong to our vendor. **We sent money to the wrong bank account.**

~

A HUGE FINANCIAL LOSS

I don't wish this on anyone. *¡A nadie!*

Believe it or not, this type of payment fraud has happened to businesses of all sizes, even including billion-dollar companies—yes, even Fortune 500 companies have had this happen. *No me digas? Te digo.* Cybercriminals are getting very sophisticated nowadays.

And while big businesses won't really feel the effect of these types of losses, we will. All the *centavitos* matter. Anytime we spend money, we want it to be well spent. It has to be an investment that'll allow our businesses to continue to grow and bring positive outcomes for the community.

That's why I'm so glad you're here and reading this book because you want to build a beautiful business. I want you to learn from others' mistakes and protect your business and your impact.

WHY DID NO ONE RING THE ALARM?

Let's dig further behind the scenes of this story. There are two key red flags here that should have sounded the alarm bells.

First, there were two requests to change bank account information in a short time period. The request isn't necessarily an uncommon action in itself—for vendors to change bank accounts—but requesting two bank account changes so close together should have raised suspicions or prompted more attention. A call should have been made directly to the vendor contact both times to confirm the change was valid and to confirm that all key information was changed. Had they done this, they would have realized the second change was not valid.

Also, the second request came via a different communication channel, via email, and the tone of the emails was less than pleasant. It was pushy, inappropriate, and disrespectful, a tone unlike the typical emails from the vendors. Any time a sense of urgency or unusual language is involved, it should prompt the recipient to check the email domains to verify the sender's identity. Had they done this, they would have realized the email domain was incorrect.

Unfortunately, neither of these red flags were detected and this business fell victim to deception and fraud.

STAY AHEAD AND VIGILANT

Payments are central to the ecosystem of your business. You buy goods or services, you get an invoice, you pay the invoice. It's a simple process.

But as you grow and scale, you have a larger volume of invoices, higher ticket invoices, and likely a team to help you do it. It becomes even more important to have the right vendor processes and protocols in place to keep up with the increasing complexity of your business. Otherwise, you'll put yourself at risk of replaying this situation in your business and falling for a scam that sends thousands to a fraudster. *Uff no, que horror.*

Plus, it's not just the money, but the time and energy that'll inevitably be required to deal with cleaning this up. (And potentially, the employee embarrassment for falling for this because no one likes to look bad. *Qué vergüenza.*)

It ultimately comes down to whether or not you would rather spend a few hours now to implement the right processes, or wait until it happens once, at which point you've lost thousands and have to implement the right processes anyway. *¿Cual prefieres?*

PROTECT YOUR HARD-EARNED MONEY

I'm hoping you prefer to prevent this from happening in the first place! With simple actions that don't cost much time or effort, you can put yourself in the best position to do so.

- **Know your vendor processes.** Especially when it comes to vendors wanting to change their bank account information, pay close attention and put in double checks (and even triple checks) for this action. Include additional scrutiny around any changes that involve cash; for instance, confirming via phone, using a small deposit confirmation to verify the bank account (i.e., deposit a few cents), or require additional approval for multiple changes in a month.

- **Never underestimate education.** With an email or short employee training, you can teach them how to spot suspicious activity by looking at email domains and identifying red flags in emails. Provide examples and a way to escalate any odd activity. And if you have the funds, consider having a professional come speak to your team on the topic. Bonus if it's during Cybersecurity Awareness Month in October.

While you can't avoid all fraud vulnerabilities, this was 100% avoidable. Taking the appropriate precautions will leave you with peace of mind that money won't slip through your hands.

P.S. We've focused here on the money aspect, but don't forget that happy vendors = happy business. If you pay your vendors the correct amount on time and send the payment to their correct bank account, operations will run efficiently and effectively. Don't risk hurting your relationship with your vendors!

They walked away with hundreds in gift cards.

POV: Engineering Manager

Apparently, this had been happening a lot.

Every day there was a new story about employees getting a text or email from our CEO telling them to buy gift cards or pay an invoice. Some would ignore it. Some would ask their team about it. Some would forward it to the IT team. Some would ask the CEO's Executive Assistant. Some would ask the CEO about it.

But, I wasn't aware this was happening.

And they got me.

Last week, I had received a text from our CEO asking for gift cards to give out at an event that they were going to that evening. Fair enough. Sounded reasonable. I was responsible for issuing gift cards from our system. It must have been urgent as they texted me directly. So I went through my process. I generated the eighteen gift cards in our system, valuing them each at $50 as instructed. I provided a link to the document with all the codes.

The next day I told my team about the request during our stand-up. They looked at me like, "Why would the CEO directly text you?" My boss looked at me strangely too. After the meeting, my boss pulled me aside and asked me for more information about it. They asked me for a copy of the text and said they would look into it.

*Later that afternoon, we got to the bottom of it. Someone had impersonated the CEO and tricked me. **They walked away with hundreds in gift cards.***

~

IMPOSTERS ARE BECOMING MORE AND MORE COMMON

This happens all too often! Texts or emails are received from imposters who're impersonating CEOs, your boss, or your colleagues. They can find out who works for your business, their title, and guess who reports to who, or who works with who. Smart, right? But we can be smarter. We can prepare for this.

At first glance, in this scenario, it might seem sufficient to speak to the employee and make sure they know what to look out for next time. We might even speak to others on their team so they know what happened and what to look out for when issuing gift cards. And all that is a good starting point.

But if we remember the root cause analysis tool that we learned about in chapter 8, we know that going down one or two why's usually doesn't get you to the heart of why something happened. The heart of it usually lies three, four, five why's down, and identifying that is what will give you the best remediation plan.

Otherwise, you risk it happening again if you don't get to the true issue. And guess what?

IT HAPPENED AGAIN

The *funny not funny* thing is that this story repeated itself a few months later.

Even though they thought it was resolved within the team responsible for issuing gift cards, there was no consideration for other scenarios where cybercriminals could find their way in. Nor were there any larger communications or education for all employees on how to watch out for cybercriminals. Only the immediate team, the CEO, and a few other people who had found out the *chisme* through the grapevine knew about what had happened.

Because of this, it was easy for the cybercriminals to slip by.

So, what happened this time? *Te cuento.* This time someone had impersonated another employee's boss and requested an invoice to be paid. And of course it had to be done immediately, so there were few questions asked.

This is why it's so important to not view negative events in a siloed manner.

THESE CYBERCRIMINALS DON'T GIVE A SH*T

These cybercriminals are finding any door to come in through. *Se meten por donde sea.*

Whether they come in posing as a vendor, as in the previous story, as the CEO, or as the employee's boss, they'll find a way to exploit vulnerabilities in your processes.

They know to emphasize time sensitivity and as soon as the transaction is executed, they know to use the gift cards right away, or know to transfer the money to another bank account immediately. It's near impossible to get it back. Once it's gone, it's gone.

These cybercriminals don't care, but we certainly do. We want our money to work for us, our business, and our communities. We need it to continue to build our dream business, so we can't take these chances. Now that we're becoming more and more friends with risk, we're better equipping ourselves to approach anything that comes our way.

Let's show those cybercriminals *quién manda aquí.*

EDUCATE YOUR EMPLOYEES

We've touched on this throughout this book, but it can't be overemphasized how critical education is as a key piece of your risk management journey. It's one of the best and most cost-effective ways to manage risks within your business overall and especially within each of your key processes.

It's much easier to do a twenty-minute presentation on cybersecurity practices than to lose tens of thousands in cash or gift cards. Train your employees on how to identify and report suspicious requests. Provide a way for them to report these events (whether it be to you, legal, IT, compliance, or a combination of all these options). Gamify it to encourage participation. The more people talk about it, the less it'll happen, if at all.

Keep your money exactly where it should be and your business growing for the long term. Don't let an imposter have your money or diminish the impact you were meant to make!

BONUS: TAKE A DEEPER DIVE

As you scale to seven figures, you'll get to a point where you want even more comfort that your business is protected. You won't want to leave yourself vulnerable.

Consider doing penetration testing (known as pen testing), which is a security exercise where a cybersecurity expert comes in and deliberately tries to find vulnerabilities. Their exercise will find gaps or weak spots in your system and where there may need to be more employee education.

They stole so much inventory from me.
POV: CEO and Founder

When I first started my business, I knew I would wear all the hats.

I also knew the first hat I would pass on would be my operations hat because it was the part I least enjoyed. I preferred all the branding and creative aspects of my business a lot more.

So when I could afford it, I hired an Operations Analyst. And when I could afford even more, I hired an Operations Manager. They had the background and expertise and were a perfect addition, especially because hiring them meant I could step away from day-to-day operations. Between the two of them, it was handled.

A year went by and we grew to the point where we could move out of my garage…and into a real warehouse! My Operations Manager, now promoted to Director, assured me it was the right move to also implement a new inventory system as part of the transition. They led the entire thing and I was grateful for it. After that, I continued to remove myself more and more from the inventory process because I trusted them fully.

One day our Operations Analyst commented that they had no more orders left to pack and was going to work on organizing the product bins. I mentioned to them that it would be great if they could help with receiving because I knew we had received many shipments that day. They responded that only the Operations Director handled receiving, and returns too. I found it odd, but didn't want to get involved.

That same week, I was reviewing the P&L and though I didn't usually look too in depth at inventory because I relied on the Operations Director, my intuition was telling me to this time. I started to replay conversations in my head where any unusual variances were explained away. And sure enough, there were a few pieces that stood out—between shipping discrepancies, inventory adjustments, and the returns accounts—something wasn't sitting right.

I started to question whether my hands-off approach had been in the best interest of my business. I hired someone to look into it. And in the end, it turned out that my intuition was right—the Operations Director had in fact been stealing inventory, reselling returns, and covering it up in the system. Now it made sense why they didn't cross-train the Operations Analyst. I felt betrayed. I lost so much money. **They stole so much inventory from me.**

~

WITHOUT SAFEGUARDS, YOU LEAVE YOURSELF VULNERABLE

Moral of the story: don't trust anyone, ever. *Broma, broma.*

In order to build your business, you have to hire. There's no way around it. You can't do it all or you'll end up overwhelmed and on your way to burnout. The risk here is that you put your full trust in your employees without implementing the right internal controls, causing you to lose thousands of dollars in inventory.

Instead, while you expand your team, you want to implement safeguards that'll be your extra set of eyes even while you're not around. That's the comfort that internal controls will give you.

SO MANY MAYBES

There might be a few ideas that come to your mind on what could have been done differently in this situation. Maybe they should have reviewed inventory more in depth. Maybe they shouldn't have lumped all inventory accounts together. Maybe they should have made sure employees were cross-trained. Maybe if they didn't place complete trust in the Operations Director or if they had cameras in the warehouse, things might have turned out differently.

There are so many "maybes," but hindsight is always 20/20.

The great news is that likely anything that you're thinking about can be turned into an internal control—a safeguard that would have prevented this altogether, or at least caught it sooner. This is what you want for your business because this way you don't have to rely on your intuition or constant oversight.

Amongst their many benefits, internal controls help protect your business from fraud. They help ensure that your business doesn't just look beautiful from the outside, but is beautiful from the inside. *Una preciosura.*

LET'S TURN SOME OF THESE MAYBES INTO INTERNAL CONTROLS

From a couple stories ago, we learned that there are both manual and automated controls that we can implement. In the inventory process, both are extremely helpful because you're dealing with how inventory is handled in the system and at the warehouse. A mix of both is a powerful defense against bad actors. Here are some examples of internal controls:

- **P&L Review** – You could review the P&L at a deeper level of detail, in this case digging into inventory accounts and questioning any transactions that are high (i.e., material) or seem unusual. (You can also delegate this, just make sure it's to someone who also doesn't have the ability to cover their tracks.)

- **Adjustments** – You could require an approval for any manual adjustments to the inventory accounts, via an adjustments form or a system approval, where the person who initiates the adjustment and the person who approves it are different. Creating this separation (i.e., segregation of duties) is a great way to protect your business.

- **Responsibilities** – You could require that all employees be cross-trained and implement a process where each employee works in each area of the warehouse at least once a month. This way you know there's a distribution of duties and one person can't hide their actions in a specific area.

- **Security** – You could install cameras at key points in the warehouse and implement a rule that inventory isn't allowed in any of the employee meal/rest areas. Even if you don't check footage, it's a deterrent for employees to know the cameras are there.

- **Counts** – You could count and reconcile against what's in your books. This can be done on a recurring basis (i.e., every week you pick a few SKUs to count) or periodic basis (i.e., every quarter/year you do a full count).

Again, these are just some examples of internal controls. There are so many within inventory that you'll eventually want to have, but it's something you want to take at your pace and capacity. For instance, as you grow, you might just need a few to simply assure you that nothing major is going awry, whereas when you start to scale, and automate, you might need a handful of them so you sleep soundly. *Sin pesadillas.*

THE FRAUD TRIANGLE

Un pequeño desvío. This story calls for the introduction of an important risk management concept—the fraud triangle—that'll help us understand more of why fraud occurs. Published by Donald R. Cressey, the **"fraud triangle" model** outlines the three conditions that can lead to fraud: motivation, opportunity, and rationalization. Essentially, it says that when all these three conditions are present from the perspective of a bad actor with access to your business, you're at risk of fraud happening to you.

So while an employee might not have thought about committing fraud previously, they might become motivated to commit fraud when faced with a life-changing event where they now are motivated by need, or maybe they feel disgruntled over something that happened at work where they feel motivated by revenge or payback. Once they're motivated, it's a quick ride to rationalization where they tell themselves all the reasons why it's okay to commit fraud and why no one will get hurt by it.

When motivation and rationalization are present for an employee, what's left is opportunity—and that's where you step in to protect your business. You don't want to give employees the opportunity to become bad actors. Even a super trusted employee could eventually betray your trust if the opportunity is there for them to take advantage of. It could be a friend who you hired, or a family member who's helping out. It could happen with anyone, and I'm sure for some of you it already has.

Whether it's day one or day 1,000, you want employees to know how things are done in your business through outlined processes and internal controls in place.

More than 50% of occupational frauds (those committed by employees) are committed due to lack of internal controls or an override of existing internal controls according to the Association of Certified Fraud Examiners.

Sold on the importance of internal controls, yet? *Ojalá que sí.*

If not, just remember that relationships can take a turn at any moment—we all remember the *telenovelas* that taught us all about *traición*.

EVALUATE YOUR INVENTORY PROCESS

Bringing it back to your inventory process, let's become friends with risk by taking some time to reflect on a few main themes from everything we've covered.

- **Where's inventory held in your books?** Is all activity lumped into one or two accounts in your accounting system or can you separate it further to give you more clarity? You don't need a ton of inventory accounts, but you should have a handful that would allow you to review and identify quickly if something major is off.

- **What adjustments do you have in inventory?** Do you know which are system-driven adjustments, and which have been recorded manually? You don't need to review every single adjustment, but consider requiring approval by you, or someone on your team, for manual adjustments above a certain threshold.

- **How are duties assigned in inventory?** Does only one person do certain activities and do they hesitate to let others take over? When employees refuse to let others carry out tasks or never take vacation days, you want to exercise caution.

- **How is your warehouse space designed?** Do you have cameras? Can theft go undetected? You want to make sure you have measures in place to know if an employee is stealing inventory.

Moral of the story: protect your inventory!

IF YOU DON'T HAVE INVENTORY

This story was very inventory heavy, but even if you don't have inventory now or never will, I want you to think about the central theme—which is that you want to avoid allowing too much power to be concentrated in the hands of one person without proper oversight.

Think about your largest assets (e.g., cash, investments, buildings, etc.) and think through where you might not have sufficient oversight, and where you might benefit from an internal control or two.

BONUS: TAKE A DEEPER DIVE

When you first start out, it's not uncommon for businesses to order and give out a ton of products and promotional samples at conferences, expos, events, influencers, campaigns, sponsorships, you name it. It's great, and often necessary, to build brand awareness and generate buzz.

But if you've scaled to the point where you're ordering thousands of dollars' worth of product every month to give away, you want to pay special attention to it. Because a fraudster doesn't always start out intending to defraud the business; it can happen innocently over time. For example, an employee might order products for an event to give to attendees. There might be a few left over, which they decide to take home for themselves and friends. Okay fine, mostly harmless. But the next time, they might add a few extra products to the order because they know they can take it home. Okay, not ideal. Eventually, they might get to the point where they think, "Wow, I have so much access to product. Let me try and sell it." Okay, we've gone too far. (This is known as products being sold on the "gray market," which is when your products are sold without authorization.)

Verify you're tracking and monitoring zero-dollar orders (e.g., you don't make money from these orders) for reasonableness as volume increases so you don't end up overlooking the fact that an employee decided to manipulate the system to their advantage. Especially when approximately 80% of businesses fail due to insufficient cash flow according to SCORE, managing your *centativos* is so, so important. You don't want to foot the bill for this.

I lost thousands by trusting them—never again.
POV: CEO and Founder

Sometimes when you know, you know.

What a horrible feeling. I grew my business from the ground up with my Executive Assistant. Now I found myself walking out of a meeting where I fired them.

I remember hiring them a couple years ago.

From the first day, they fit right in with our team. They were dedicated, experienced, and quick on their feet. They did all the things I needed and more— had my calendar sorted at all times, moved meetings at a moment's notice, booked my travel, and always brought my coffee the way I liked it. They kept me from dealing with administrative tasks and sometimes would even take on additional tasks so I could focus on the business. I remember one time they said, "Why don't we send a welcome gift to all visitors or prospective clients?" I loved that idea, so they got trained on how to place orders and took it on moving forward.

Over time, they would sit in on important meetings with me so that they knew how to handle to-dos and next steps. I even eventually started handing over tasks that they would handle on my behalf; for instance, handing over the reins of approving expenses for all my direct reports. I was happy they took initiative and even happier to hand it off. At the time, I did ask myself if I should still do a review, but again, I figured they had it covered. They even took my own expense report off my hands.

Oh, and there was one time I gave them access to our bank account for an emergency payment that they offered to help with.

Fast forward to today, they were fired.

Those orders we allowed them to make for welcome gifts—well, they were placing orders for themselves multiple times a month.

Those expense reports I trusted them with—well, they were submitting all their own expenses as if it was their personal expense account.

That bank account I had given them access to—well, they still had access and they had been transferring $700 to themselves every month.

I lost thousands by trusting them—never again.

~

EXECUTIVE ASSISTANTS HAVE A LOT OF POWER

Executive Assistants (EAs) are lifesavers! Shoutout to all the EAs that do so much for executives and their businesses. I don't know how they do it.

But like any employee, if you give them keys to the kingdom, your kingdom, you have to make sure you're proactively looking out for yourself and your business. With the level of access EAs typically have to execute key actions like ordering products, accessing expense systems, and approving cash transfers, they have a lot of power.

You don't want to risk giving too much access to them and definitely not without sufficient oversight. If you think about the fraud triangle that we introduced in the previous story, this EA had so many opportunities to commit fraud that it's not a surprise they eventually were tempted by the many ways they could exploit the business. Whether they were a bad actor coming in or not, they fell into temptation when given access to cash and product.

IT'S ALL ABOUT WHAT COULD GO WRONG

This doesn't mean we have to constantly doubt our employees, question their every move, or accuse them of wrongdoing. *Nada que ver.*

It does mean that you want to design processes that allow you to feel confident and safe in your business. *Tienes que protegerte.*

A great way to do this is to ask yourself **what could go wrong (WCGW)**. This is another useful concept in the risk management world that helps you understand what a process should look like, or evaluate where an existing process might have gaps. Because when you ask yourself WCGW, you can reverse engineer how to prevent it from happening by developing a process that avoids giving those negative events the opportunity to occur.

And the earlier you implement it, the better ingrained it becomes in your process and the more objectively it's viewed. In other words, if you implement it up-front, the employee walks into the business with the process already in place. The process is the process. But if you add something later, the employee might think it's only there to monitor them because you don't trust them.

The WCGW concept could have been useful in this story because it would have prompted the CEO to set up the processes differently.

PREVENTATIVE OR DETECTIVE—YOU DECIDE

As we've highlighted throughout this book, the wonderful thing about risk management is that you have an abundance of choice when it comes to how you want to manage it. It's about becoming friends with risk your way. *A tu manera y de nadie más.*

Once you identify WCGW, you can put measures in place to prevent it from going wrong. You can use a preventative approach, a detective approach, or a combination of both. Whereas a preventative approach will prevent it from happening in the first place, a detective approach will detect it after the fact, but ideally before it becomes a big issue.

Most businesses will typically find a balance of the two that works for them. It'll ultimately depend on your risk appetite and tolerance, your resources, and how much desire you have to squash WCGW.

TAKING A PREVENTATIVE APPROACH

Let's apply a preventive approach to this story.

The placing of orders—the CEO could have had the EA work with the Sales or Customer Service team to place them, instead of giving them direct access to the system. (Anytime you give direct access to a system, or a transaction, to someone who doesn't necessarily need it, or maybe even know how to do it, you expose yourself to fraud or human error.)

The expense reports—they could have had the EA prepare and do a preliminary review of expenses reports, but they could have still retained final review and approval of the expense reports. (They could have even given the EA their own card to better track.)

The bank account withdrawals—they should have had the access removed immediately after the emergency payment. (Special circumstances might come up, but you want to highly scrutinize and monitor any access to bank accounts that's granted.)

TAKING A DETECTIVE APPROACH

You might be thinking that—if this were you—you would still give them access to everything above. You want them to be able to place orders, you want them to have access to the bank account, and you want them to submit and approve expense reports. It's easier and faster on a day-to-day basis for your business.

Well, I'd tell you that's all good, *me parece bien*. I'd tell you that instead, you can take a detective approach, so you can catch any errors before they become major problems for your business.

The placing of orders—the CEO could have set it up to where they (or someone else appropriate) received a report of all the orders the EA placed that quarter to scan for anything unusual.

The expense reports—they could have set up a process where quarterly the accounting team reviewed business expenses for any significant, duplicate, or fraudulent expenses.

The bank account withdrawals—they could have (and should already have had) a process in place to do bank reconciliations to reconcile activity every month. They could have specifically called out to the accounting team to review any manual transfers.

Again, this doesn't mean that the mistakes, errors, or potential fraud won't happen, but you'll catch it quickly so you can take swift action to correct.

And if you're short on time, or have high risk tolerance, leverage the concept of thresholds where you only review unusual items above a certain amount (not everything needs to be checked to death).

What approach would you take in this scenario? Do you think you would lean toward a preventative or detective approach, or a mix of both?

ANALYZE YOUR ACCESS POINTS

Become friends with risk by knowing how much access you give to each employee in all your key processes, especially those that have access to high-impact actions (e.g., access to cash, access to product,) or those that have the opportunity to bypass certain protocols.

In your own business, reflect on your key access points. Here are three to get you started:

- **Placing Orders** – Who has access to place orders in your business? Does it make sense? Do they need it? Can you simplify the process so it's easy for you to check?

- **Approving Expense Reports** – How do you handle expense reports? Who reviews and approves them? Who gets reimbursed and for what? Is there a policy or a system that's setting the ground rules and enforcing them?

- **Withdrawing Cash** – Who has access to your bank accounts? What kind of access do they have? And are you reconciling cash at least quarterly in a way that would capture suspicious activity?

Trust, but verify. You can't have eyes everywhere, but by managing the risks, you can have more assurance that things are running as they should, and in your favor.

Part 4

TRANSFORMATION

Chapter 10

Evolve Your Business: Outdated Infrastructure Can Prevent Your Business from Transforming into Its Next Version

Your business will change over time. Year one won't look like year two, which won't look like year seven. As sales increase, as finances become more complex, as systems are added, your infrastructure will be pressure tested and it'll require your business to go through several transformations so that it can step into its new version each time. In this chapter, we'll talk about what risks you'll encounter and how you can move through each stage—emerging, growing, scaling—in a way that successfully propels your beautiful business forward.

I wasn't ready for the next level.
POV: CEO and Founder

When I started this business, I had no idea where it would go.

To be honest, I saw a need and I created a solution that worked for me. I told others what I was doing and they wanted in. They were having the same issues and this solution worked for them too.

We grew initially by word of mouth and organic marketing. We sold at pop-up markets and attended larger expos if we could. I'll never forget our first expo—it was a collaborative effort between us and a few other businesses because our budgets weren't enough to put us in those spaces on our own, yet. We were scrappy, but it worked for us.

Little by little, we grew, and our brand was being recognized more.

A couple years in, we competed in a pitch competition and won! The award was a one-year contract with a PR agency. We knew this would elevate us to the next level. We talked about the buzz that would be created and how that would generate sales. We talked about what that would mean for our growth and the investments that we could make with the additional revenue. And by we, I mean myself and a few others because our team was still small. I was still wearing most of the hats, so everything still went through me.

What we didn't talk about, or prepare for, was what the additional traffic would do to our operations. And for the most part, I'll admit that we were okay throughout the year as each feature debuted and sales came in. We made it work.

But one morning we were featured in a major publication. It was with such high praise that sales came rolling in—more than we'd ever seen before. It put pressure on everything: our systems, our processes, our team, and me. So much so that we crashed.

Our systems couldn't handle the capacity and shut down. Our inventory ran out and we couldn't fulfill all our orders. I crashed too. I had a hand in so much—too much. I came to a scary realization. **I wasn't ready for the next level.**

~

WHEN A WIN ISN'T A WIN

Guau, what began as a great PR feature turned into chaos. *Una desgracia total*.

We might think that a win is always a win, but sometimes it's not. This seemingly amazing PR feature ended up breaking down their business operations and harming their image.

The CEO relied on their "we'll make it work" approach, instead of pressure testing their back-end operations and spending some more time preparing for what could happen. And to their surprise, they fell short and it blew up in their face.

GREAT PROBLEMS TO HAVE ARE STILL PROBLEMS

Sometimes we think that as soon as we get a specific opportunity, achieve a certain goal, or pass a revenue milestone—we've made it. That suddenly the path will become clear, our problems will disappear, and everything will figure itself out.

But the truth is that it's nothing like that.

Because the more your business grows, the more your team expands, the more opportunities you're presented with, and the more accolades you receive, it means more of everything. More of the good and also the bad.

You have much more at stake and added pressure to perform.

That client you landed after a year of relationship building—now make sure you can deliver. That retailer you landed after working at it for so long—now make sure your operations can support it. That collaboration you landed after dreaming about it for months—now make sure you can hold up your end.

This story is a perfect example of what happens when you don't anticipate the risks that come with seemingly amazing opportunities, which is where great problems to have can just turn into problems if you don't proactively manage risks.

If today you landed a feature to be in a major publication, speak on a morning talk show, or pitch on a well-known TV show, would your business be ready? Are there any opportunities that you're currently contemplating saying yes or no to?

THE PPT FRAMEWORK IS YOUR SECRET WEAPON

PPT stands for people, process, and technology.

While the model has changed over time by those who have used it or adapted it, the **PPT framework** is particularly helpful when building out your business foundations and handling significant changes in your business as you transform, which is why I've waited to introduce it until part 4. (It can also be applied to many of the scenarios we explored in the other stories. It helps any time you're making decisions on your operations at a high level, for a specific process or for an initiative.)

People, process, and technology are the three elements that work in unison to successfully support your beautiful business. Together, they help you chart the right path toward a business goal, map out the right solution to overcome a potential obstacle (as in this story), or even help you recover from setbacks. PPT supports you as you make decisions in your business. *Es tu apoyo.*

So, what exactly do I mean by PPT and how should you apply it? Let's walk through it.

- **People – This is all about the people involved.** Who are they? Are they all aware of the role they play? Are they all on board with it? Do you need more resources, whether temps, contractors, or full-time hires?

- **Process – This is all about the processes involved.** Which processes are affected? Are they documented? Are they consistent? Do you need to update them, document them in the first place, or revise them? Do you need to train your people on them?

- **Technology – This is all about your systems.** What systems are you using, if any? Are they set up well? Will they support you? Or do you need to implement something new that'll better support you?

Applying it to the story here, there should have been a massive pressure test of their operations using these three elements. If they had brainstormed and run scenarios of how their PPT could have been affected by the PR feature, they would have found that there was a disconnect that could lead to a failure. They would have been able to find a risk response they were comfortable with, and execute on it. Instead, it wreaked havoc on their business.

If only they had known the importance of seeing their business through a risk lens, and to use the PPT framework, they would have been much better prepared as their business evolved.

DAY ONE WON'T LOOK LIKE DAY 1,700

Zooming out, no business that's around for years will run the same way it did on day one. The truth is that a successful business will continue to outgrow and transform itself over time, and that's perfectly normal and needed.

To be an effective leader, you need to know how to evolve your business through each of its versions. For simplicity's sake, we'll say your business goes through three main stages as it transforms: emerging, growing, and scaling. Let's apply the PPT framework to outline how your business foundations and risk approach might look at each stage.

- **Emerging – Your goal in the emerging stage is to keep PPT simple so you don't risk overcomplicating your business before it's time.**

  In the beginning, you just want your business to run. You want to market, sell, and collect payment for a product that customers want. You'll likely be a team of one, or a small team, and employ some contractors. You'll want to keep your primary processes documented. You'll also want to keep your systems and automations simple up front. Manual spreadsheets will work just fine for many of the tasks your business needs. Don't convince yourself—or let someone sell you on—needing a bunch of people, multiple processes, or all the systems and automations. As an emerging business, let yourself enjoy this stage without all the complexity.

- **Growing – Your goal in the growing stage is to elevate PPT intentionally so you don't risk moving too fast in your business as you expand.**

  As you grow, you want your business to be able to handle the increased capacity. You want to expand your product and develop customer loyalty. You'll start to add more employees and contractors, and divide into a few teams. You'll also want to document your secondary processes and work with your team to keep them updated. This is when you'll start to integrate a few other helpful systems and automations because you have the need and the funds to do so. Plus, you'll begin to delegate more of your work because your capacity will have shifted. This is when you'll decide whether to offload work to a person, automate it with a system, or a combination of both. Don't become the bottleneck during your growing phase. Focus on finding systems that fit your size. As a growing business, let yourself experiment and shape your business without tying yourself to a fixed plan.

- **Scaling – Your goal in the scaling stage is to make PPT streamlined so you don't risk preventing your business from reaching its potential.**

   As you scale, you want your business to be repeatable, routine, and streamlined. You want to cement your place in your industry and deliver outstanding customer value. You'll need to revisit all your people, processes, and systems. You'll expand your team even further, adding multiple departments, bringing in some of your outsourced work in-house, and identifying areas where you need subject-matter expertise. You'll want to document all your processes and validate that they're running consistently in your business. This is also when you might replace some of your systems because you want to ensure they can handle your business size and transaction volume. And you'll want to start thinking further out—for instance, five years with your PPT. Don't underestimate the importance of reevaluating everything and letting go of what doesn't serve you, including certain revenue streams (e.g., where personalized products may have been okay before, they may not be worth it now). As a scaling business, it's important that you periodically break down your business, and release any customized chaos to make way for long-term magic.

Poquito a poquito, you'll lay out great foundations for your business. As your business shifts, embrace the new challenges and PPT that are required to further strengthen your foundations. Don't rush it. Witnessing your business transform into something beautiful and evolve over time is truly special.

I believe in you. *¡Sí, se puede!*

REFLECT ON YOUR STAGE

This was a lot of information for the first story of part 4. *Inhala, exhala.*

Reflect on what stage you're in currently. Is it emerging, growing, or scaling? If you think about your PPT right now, does it match where you want to be? Are there adjustments you want to make? Make a list of three key actions that called out to you, and make a plan to execute them over the next year. Your beautiful business awaits.

BONUS: TAKE A DEEPER DIVE

One thing that definitely will change from day one to day 1,700 is the number of meetings you have. If I had a dollar for every person who has said they spend way too much time in meetings...*sería millonaria.*

When you're emerging, it's really easy for you to be in all meetings, so when you grow or scale, it can be hard to let go of the practice. But putting it into perspective, every time you have a meeting, you're taking away from your team being able to execute. An "only one hour" weekly status meeting that six people come to isn't just one hour, it's SIX hours every week that could have been spent working on your business. And when we need to maximize the time we have, and the dollars we pay to have that time, this doesn't serve us. We risk not moving the needle in our businesses because we're stuck in meetings!

As you grow and scale, be careful to not let meetings become an overwhelming part of you and your team's day. Some tips: Schedule a meeting with a clear purpose and invite only those that need to be in the discussion. Delegate a meeting that can be handled by your team. Or avoid a meeting altogether if it can be resolved via a quick message or voice note. And please don't make meetings recurring unless necessary.

Challenge yourself to review the length, attendees, and purpose of your meetings so you can make it to your next level with ease. And give your employees a safe space to question this as well.

I thought my numbers made sense.
POV: CEO and Founder

Things were going well for us on the funding front.

While we had initially bootstrapped, once our customers loved us and recommended us to their friends, sales grew, and we were able to access other options. In addition to reinvesting our profits, we could now tap into loans and seek out investors to fund our business. Each time we got funding from loans or investors, we had to go through the due diligence process—the not-so-fun but required part of business. We provided them with all the necessary financials and documentation to get approved.

The first time we got a loan, it went well. We had a simple business model, so it was easy to get everything together. We had a good handle on our numbers.

The second time we sought funding from investors, it still went well, but it took more time. We were much larger and had expanded our business model beyond services to also include online courses, which required us to add another platform. Pulling from two systems wasn't too bad. We still had full confidence in our financials.

Shortly after, we hit the seven-figure mark and we started to evolve even further. We had centralized into a new financial system that pulled data from the other systems. That implementation was rough to say the least, but it seemed to be working okay. We also added a payroll and an employee expense reimbursement system. However, I did notice it took longer to generate financials than I expected. If I asked for them, it would take a week to get them and I would only receive a summary page without much detail.

Maybe it was growing pains, but I definitely had less confidence in our numbers than before.

The next time we presented to investors, we were hit hard. It was a sizable investment we were seeking, so naturally they asked a lot of questions about our financials. I defended our numbers, but wasn't able to answer all the questions they had. They found holes in what we stated as actuals and what we were projecting in our forecast. To move forward, they asked for underlying data and assumptions. My team provided some of the supporting reports, but not all the underlying data matched, especially in our current year actuals. In one way or another, basically every number we had in our financials was off—and a few of our assumptions didn't even have a valid rationale.

Here I thought we were doing well by generating more sales, adding revenue streams, and implementing new systems, but now we found ourselves looking bad to funders. We needed to clean this sh*t up. My business looked like a horrible investment now. How did I get here? **I thought my numbers made sense.**

~

YOU MIGHT NOT LIKE THIS PART

Los numeros, uff. If you have always avoided numbers, working with them might make you want to scream. Even if you have some understanding of them and have worked with them in the past, it's still daunting. And even if you like or love numbers, you might be realizing you can't spend all your time focused on them because you need to lead your business as its CEO.

We might not have set out to have to deal with numbers as much as we do in our business—but no matter how you feel about them—you don't have a business if you don't know your numbers. It's critical to develop an understanding of your finances, even if it's boring or doesn't come natural to you. The reality is that if you don't have a profitable business, you can't impact the way you want to.

YOUR NUMBERS TELL A STORY

When it comes down to it, your numbers tell a story—the story of your business. And we love a good story. ¡Nos gusta el chisme!

In business, your story is told through the lens of financials, shorthand for financial statements, which are three statements.

- **Income Statement – Your income statement captures your business activity over a specific period of time.** It shows your revenue (i.e., how much money you've made), expenses (i.e., how much money you've spent), and profit (i.e., what's left over). Revenue and expenses can be broken out further by type to tell a more detailed story, and typically profit will also be viewed from three different angles—after paying for your product, after operating expenses, and finally, after taxes.

- **Balance Sheet – Your balance sheet is a snapshot of your business at one moment in time.** It shows your assets (i.e., what you own—cash, investments, accounts receivable, etc.), your liabilities (i.e., what you owe—loans, accounts payable, gift cards), and your equity (i.e., what's left over after you pay your liabilities). This is the value remaining for you and your shareholders. Assets = Liabilities + Equity.

- **Statement of Cash Flows – Your statement of cash flows is what it sounds like—it shows how your cash has flowed from one period to another.** It outlines how you used cash in your business. Cash can be made or spent in three categories: operating activities (e.g., collecting cash from customers), investing activities (e.g., spending cash on equipment), or financing activities (e.g., receiving cash from a loan or investor). The first two statements can hide pieces of the story sometimes. This statement helps fill in the gaps.

These statements can be actual or projected, with actual being what has already occurred in your business, and projected being an estimate of future results given your current conditions, assumptions, and plans. You need both to operate a beautiful business.

Financials tell the full story of your business's performance. The truth may be hard to face at times, but what matters most is that you know where you stand so you can move forward with eyes wide open.

This is what will allow you to confidently make decisions, whether that be to continue as is, or adjust a few things—for example, add a revenue stream, hire someone, invest in equipment, or cancel a subscription. You might even pivot completely, to change the direction of your story.

And you certainly don't want to tell a fake story as they did here. Instead of properly vetting their sources and fact-checking their claims, they let their story run wild. Their financials didn't make sense and it cost them their funding.

The last thing you want is to misrepresent your business. You don't want to risk finding yourself in the news, or worse—being brought up on charges for presenting false information that collapses your business.

¡Ponte las pilas! Always maintain your financial integrity.

TWO KEY CALLOUTS

Do you want the good news or the (kinda) bad news first?

Bad? Okay.

No matter your stage, you're ultimately responsible for keeping your story truthful. Because while you can, and should, put measures in place and form a support system to assist you, the onus falls on you for maintaining your financial integrity with accurate financials. You can't pass this on even if you're a multimillion-dollar business. This is how you protect your business, its reputation, and the impact you'll have. *¿Aceptas esta responsabilidad?*

Now the good news—you're not responsible for being accurate to the penny. It's not about matching every *centavito*. Your financials should be "reasonably accurate," meaning that they're not misleading and can be relied on to make decisions about your business. (As a career auditor can tell you, a.k.a. me, we aren't seeking perfection. We simply want things to be reasonably accurate so that key stakeholders know how the business is doing.)

YOUR FINANCIAL ECOSYSTEM

What you do to manage your finances, maintain financial integrity, and mitigate your financial risks will look different based on your stage and will evolve with your business.

So, what should you do in your business?

As you learned in the last story, a helpful way to think about how to map out solutions is in terms of the PPT framework. While it's fresh in our minds, let's use it again here to assess your financial ecosystem at each stage.

- **Emerging – Your goal in the emerging stage is to keep PPT simple so you don't risk overcomplicating your business before it's time.** In the beginning, it's easier to keep track of your finances because you have a simple business model and a lower number of transactions. You're just trying to turn a profit! You'll be fine doing things on your own, or if it's not your forte or you just don't want to spend time doing it yourself, you can hire contractors like a consultant to help you design your projections and analyze actuals or a bookkeeper to help keep your numbers in order. Contractors are great at this stage because you can lean on expertise without having to bring someone on full time. As far as process, you'll mainly rely on your contractors' processes. You might keep a simple process for what you do on your end to review your financials (e.g., a quarterly review), and how you ensure your financials are reasonably accurate (e.g., revenue, expenses, cash, inventory, etc.). A financial system is optional at this point depending on what you feel comfortable with, and where you want to dedicate your energy (it takes time and energy to learn a system no matter how easy it's portrayed to be).

- **Growing – Your goal in the growing stage is to elevate PPT intentionally so you don't risk moving too fast in your**

business as you expand. As you grow, you expand your business model and the volume of transactions increases. You're focused on growing revenue in line with your expenses! This is the stage where if you haven't hired contractors, you should unless you really have expertise in finances or love to do it. As your operations become larger, consider bringing on a finance lead or a fractional CFO to handle your projections and actuals, and upgrading your Bookkeeper to an Accountant that has more expertise. From a process perspective, document your key finance processes because it'll serve you now and for when you decide it's time to hire. You'll need to understand your process for reviewing financials and key metrics (such as through a monthly review or a finance KPI report) and how this process ensures that your financials are reasonably accurate at the next level of detail (like by revenue stream, expense type, short-term vs. long-term, etc.). At this point, if you haven't already, you'll want to implement a financial system, but be sure to seek out one that fits your business.

- **Scaling – Your goal in the scaling stage is to make PPT streamlined so you don't risk preventing your business from reaching its potential.** As you scale, it's time to revisit all your people, processes, and technology. You're focused on growing revenue faster than your expenses! At this stage, you should delegate everything if you haven't already, as you can no longer dedicate the necessary time to them while also leading everything else. You'll elevate your financial ecosystem by having people with increased experience and credentials. It's also a good idea to fully separate your finance and accounting teams if you haven't already. And while you can still have a fractional CFO at this stage who's a contractor, make sure you have a plan to get a full-time CFO. As for your accounting team, you'll want to hire a controller and a few accountants, some with their CPA license. From a process perspective, you'll want to document all your finance processes. You'll want to know how you review financials, key metrics, and key reports (e.g., a monthly review, a financial KPI report, and a daily revenue report), and have a plan to validate whether everything is working as intended, especially where assumptions or judgments are involved. This is when you'll reevaluate and likely upgrade your financial system for one that suits your business size, transaction volume, and offers additional integrations with other systems you use. Take extra time to ensure the system is working the way it should, that data is integrated properly, and that any reports you pull are complete and accurate with the right parameters. This is the stage when you'll read everything again with the context of financial integrity. Break down your business and release what doesn't serve you!

The PPT framework sets you up for success. Your financial ecosystem isn't a place where you want creativity to run wild.

A WORD OF CAUTION

Remember that the culture you maintain in your business will dictate a lot of what can happen in your business. If you maintain a very strong culture and tone at the top that leads with integrity, it'll trickle down to your financial integrity. Employees will be less likely to push numbers toward a certain direction because they feel pressure to, or need to in order to keep their bonus or position.

And the stronger internal controls that you have, the more employees will know they can't trick you into thinking things are better than they are. They won't be able to fluff them up, or purposely leave out information that should be included.

THE DREADED TAXES

I haven't really mentioned taxes yet for two reasons—first, this was already a lot of information, and second, no one likes taxes—but I'm going to give taxes their time in the spotlight now for a quick minute. *Por un minuto solamente.*

Long story short, finance, accounting, and taxes all play a part in your numbers and your financial ecosystem. With taxes, you want to do three things: (1) Set aside a certain percentage for taxes from revenue that comes in every month, (2) Pay estimated taxes every quarter, and (3) File taxes every year with a qualified tax preparer, who may or may not be a CPA (not all CPAs do taxes). And if you have the funds and the time, invest in tax planning during the year to create a tax strategy that works for you.

WHAT'S YOUR CURRENT FINANCIAL ECOSYSTEM?

Based on your stage, what does your financial ecosystem look like? Take a moment to map it out in terms of PPT. Are you happy with where you are, or do you want to make some adjustments?

And if you had to rate your financial integrity, where would you rate it on a scale of one to ten? One being, "I have no idea," or, "I'm confident it's not right," and ten being, "I know our financials are correct to the penny." Anywhere from eight to ten passes. If you're anywhere below an eight, reflect on how you can get your rating up.

BONUS: TAKE A DEEPER DIVE

If you're ever thinking about going public—one of the most significant transformations a business can go through—your financial integrity is a critical area you'll have to focus on. There'll be even more scrutiny over your numbers. You'll receive evaluations on how well you manage your financial risks and you'll start hearing words like "deficiency," "significant deficiency," and "material weakness" that'll indicate there are things to be fixed. Ensure you're adequately prepared and seek out expertise for a readiness assessment. More diverse founders taking their business public—that would be kick-a**!

I failed to plan, so I guess I planned to fail.
POV: HR Manager

It was clear that something needed to be done.

As soon as I came on board, I started noticing things about how employees were spending the business's money. I noticed that meal expenses for team celebrations and entertaining potential clients had gone up. I noticed that travel to events, conferences, and expos had gone up. I noticed that there were gifts given for anything and everything. The occasional splurge—fine—but it was apparent that there were no limits, nor was there consistency in how employees decided what was acceptable and relevant to the business.

And it wasn't just the cost, but I was also hearing things about how "so and so" team was allowed to spend more money, and how "so and so" leader was allowed to spend more. "Why did they get to do happy hour every week, and my team only got to do it once every few months?" "Why did they stay at a five-star hotel, and we had to stay at a three-star hotel?"

Not to mention that I heard an earful from accounting on how processing these expenses was a mess. Some employees provided receipts, some didn't. Some provided a business purpose for the expense, some didn't. Some submitted expense reports in a timely fashion, some hadn't submitted expense reports for months, and had to be chased by accounting to do so.

I wanted to change it. It was clear to me that we were headed for disaster and resentment. I wanted to make the experience better all around by doing an overhaul of how we approached employee spend, including bringing in a new system to help automate the process. I presented the idea to my boss and got the green light for my employee spend initiative. Once finance had approved my budget, I went full steam ahead to execute my idea, building everything out, and providing a few updates to my boss here and there. And I had a couple quick conversations with accounting, but I'll admit that most of the initiative lived in my head.

I figured we would do full training on it once it was done so employees could adopt it. Easy peasy.

*But it was far from it. After pouring months into this project, when it was finally ready to go live, I communicated the changes at our town hall, and basically felt like tomatoes were being thrown at me. No one knew about it. Everyone had questions. It didn't go over well. I should have anticipated how it would be received. **I failed to plan, so I guess I planned to fail.***

~

A GOAL WITHOUT A PLAN IS JUST A WISH

It doesn't matter how well-intentioned you are—if you don't have a plan, you're setting yourself up for potential failure.

The HR Manager had a wish to make the employee experience better. They saw the risk of employees spending too much, which could affect profitability. They saw the risk of employees spending inconsistently, which could affect the culture. They saw the risk of employees spending without guidance, which could cause confusion.

However, they fell short when it came time for execution. No matter what the problems were with the existing way of doing things, it was still the existing way of doing things, and employees were used to that. And people resist change. *Sabemos esto.*

¡Aguántate! Before you decide to skip this part because employee spend may not apply to you—though you should know me better by now—this applies to any projects, especially large-scale initiatives, that affect your business as a whole.

SIX STEPS TO MAKING A PROJECT PLAN

When you decide it's time to undertake large-scale initiatives that'll transform your business, you want to make sure you have all your bases covered before beginning. You want to take into account all relevant factors and get input from all the stakeholders involved. If not, you risk executing a project that ends up failing. And it wastes valuable time, money, and energy. *No queremos esto.*

So, what do you do? Follow my **six-step project plan** to prepare every project for success.

- **Step 1 – Identify the project manager and project sponsor.** Who will be in charge of managing and overseeing this project? This might be you and someone on your team, or it might be you identifying who will take on both of these roles if you're delegating it.

- **Step 2 – Brainstorm all stakeholders that need to be involved in the project.** Take a wide sweep of your business and determine who should have input and who will be affected by this initiative. Is it legal, accounting, HR, communications, IT, finance? And if it'll affect all employees, identify a few that should join the project team.

- **Step 3 – Bring everyone together to discuss the project plan.** Once the project manager has drafted the first version of the project plan with the project purpose, objectives, key steps, final deliverables, timeline, and go-live date, set up a planning meeting with stakeholders to discuss. Allow stakeholders to contribute and brainstorm. Start to divide up key steps and assign responsibilities. If there are any new stakeholders identified, follow up with them after and get them up to speed.

- **Step 4 – Align on the final project plan and deliverables.** Hold any other planning meetings needed until everyone agrees to the final project plan and deliverables that'll make this project a success. Make sure the project plan has all the steps needed to get to the final deliverable; for instance, is there a system that has to be sourced, designed, and tested first? Make sure the final deliverables are complete as well. In the case of a new system, it's not just the system that's the deliverable, but also the user guide or video training that goes along with it.

- **Step 5 – Determine how the project will be communicated.** A communication approach is one of the most invaluable pieces of a successful project. How will you communicate about this project, all the way up to and on the go-live date? During the project, this might be via emails, regular status meetings, or a messaging channel. For go-live, this might look like a town hall, a leadership meeting, a staff meeting, an email, a training, and/or a self-paced course. There are so many ways to do this. What matters is that everyone involved in or affected by the project is on the same page.

- **Step 6 – Evaluate what monitoring is needed, if any.** Will the project need any ongoing monitoring, or need to be revisited after a period of time? It could be a monthly or quarterly check-in to see how everything is going. It could be a twelve-month revisit to see if anything significant needs to change, which can be helpful for a decision you made and aren't sure if you want it to be permanent. It could be a feedback form to see how employees are feeling about it, or an audit to see if things are working as they should.

¡Y listo! Having a project plan will help you think through everything, connect all the dots, and get the buy-in you need to take the project across the finish line. Become friends with risk by planning each project appropriately, especially large-scale initiatives that require multiple stakeholders and analysis from several angles. Don't make the mistake of not having one for large-scale initiatives!

RACI CHART TO THE RESCUE

A great pairing for the project plan is a great RACI chart. It would have rescued this employee spend initiative because it's perfect for cross-functional projects that involve many people and multiple departments.

A **RACI chart** helps outline exactly which roles belong to whom for each step and each deliverable you've identified in your project plan. It also helps keep your project on track and prevents miscommunication. Often, it'll help move the project along if there's indecision or if there are conflicting opinions, because you know who has ultimate say.

So, what does RACI stand for?

- **R is for Responsible** – This is the person who's responsible for developing and completing the specified project step or deliverable. They may be doing this on their own, or they may have a team to help them execute. (If there's a team that's responsible, an R* can be used to designate the lead responsible person.)

- **A is for Accountable** – This is the person who's accountable for each project step or deliverable. They ultimately have authority, so there should only be one of them. This helps move decisions along if a project step or deliverable is stuck.

- **C is for Consulted** – These are the people who will provide guidance during the project. It could be communications, legal, IT, HR, or marketing depending on the project.

- **I is for Informed** – These are the people who don't need to be in the day-to-day meetings, but do need to stay in the loop with any major project updates.

A RACI chart may seem *un poco complicado* at first, but once you get the hang of it, it'll help any large-scale initiatives you have in your business go much more smoothly.

SIZE MATTERS

I want to take a minute to mention that I'm not advocating for you to apply a project plan and RACI chart to every single one of your projects. These tools are not meant to slow down your business with structure and rigidity, but to provide you with ways to amplify your success and reduce the risk of failures. These tools are mainly for the large-scale projects and transformations where there's significant risk if the project doesn't go well. (Though if you love them—by all means, feel free to use them everywhere.)

Depending on the size of your project, you can use a modified version of these tools or skip them altogether. For instance, if the project is for your Social Media Coordinator to create a new standard operating procedure (SOP) around how to post on a specific social media platform, you can simply assign it to them and get it done. You don't need a detailed project plan or RACI chart. Or if the project is to implement a new system that only affects the accounting team, then you might use a simplified version of the project plan and skip the RACI chart. But if the project is to bring a new product to market, this is a large-scale initiative that you would need a detailed project plan and RACI chart approach for.

The same principles apply for team size. The way you approach a project will depend on whether you're a team of one, a team of seven, or a team of eighty-seven. It ultimately depends on what you're comfortable with, what the likelihood of failure is, and how much risk you're willing to take on.

BACK TO EMPLOYEE SPEND

As you might anticipate, similar to our last two stories, what your employee spend approach looks like will depend on what stage you're in.

In your emerging stage, you're likely a team of one, or a small team, so it's okay to keep things simple with your employee spend approach. If you do have a few employees, you can encourage them to spend smart and trust their judgment. You can use manual spreadsheets for expense reimbursement. And you'll be able to see any unusual spend quickly, which can be brought to their attention. Your large-scale initiatives are likely in other areas.

As you enter your growing stage, it'll make sense to outline employee spend principles, and document high-level processes and procedures. You might consider adding a system to start bringing automations into the process if your team is large enough and is often incurring spend on their own. This might warrant a simplified version of the project plan to bring it to life.

Once you hit the scaling stage, you'll definitely want to execute a large-scale initiative around employee spend, which includes a travel & expense (T&E) policy, process, and system that aligns your business. Leverage a project plan and RACI chart to ensure all the important pieces of your employee spend initiative are captured, executed, and monitored. Remember that in the scaling stage, you want repeatable, routine, and streamlined efforts that'll allow you to rely on your setup as opposed to you having to worry if everything is working correctly.

WHAT'S YOUR NEXT LARGE-SCALE INITIATIVE?

What's your next large-scale initiative that aims to transform your business? Is it adding a new service, rebranding an existing product line, implementing a new system, moving to a new office, or expanding internationally?

Pick your most significant initiative and apply my six-step project plan and/or the RACI chart to mitigate the risk of failure and ensure it's ready for success.

BONUS: TAKE A DEEPER DIVE

When you're in the scaling stage, you'll also want to incorporate fraud risk considerations as you execute new projects. You'll want to identify any internal controls that would make anything unusual or unexpected to pop out. With employee spend, some examples you could consider include having expenses reports above a specific dollar amount reviewed, adding an additional approval for certain types of expenses, or conducting audits on a sample of employee expense reports.

Chapter 11

Bring Your Employees Along: Without Collaborative Communication and Intentional Hiring, You May Not Transform the Way You Envisioned

As you expand your team, you enter a whole new world that requires you to manage and lead people. It becomes critical that you actively think about how and when you'll hire employees, and then once they're on board, how you'll communicate and collaborate with them, especially during significant change in your business so they embrace it rather than reject it. The better your talent approach is, the better you'll be at preventing layoffs or rapid turnover. In this chapter, we'll address how to leverage a risk lens to intentionally develop and maintain one of your biggest assets: your people.

My employees didn't need to know.
POV: Director of Operations

I was incredibly happy when I got the call. It was a dream role.

I was going to be the new Director of Operations at a beverage company that was growing fast. I had so many ideas and changes that I wanted to make. Based on my interviews, we were going to need new systems, new people, new processes—a full overhaul. The prior Director of Operations had been there for several years, and in my opinion, it was time for a big change to get the business ready for its next version. I was ready to hit the ground running my first week.

I met with each member of my team, as well as several other department heads. We talked about their challenges, and I shared my background and the expertise I was bringing to the role. These conversations helped confirm what I wanted to do, and I wasted no time.

I started to make changes the following week. Some were communicated via email—a simple, "Hey, this is what we're doing now, effective as of this date." Some changes I communicated via a quick meeting—a simple, "Hey, this has changed. Make sure you adopt it." The biggest change I held an hour meeting for. I unveiled the grand vision for our new system, which we would implement over the next six months. I instructed my team members on key processes that would change, like how we sourced ingredients and how we fulfilled orders.

With all these changes, everyone was mostly quiet, which I naïvely took as a sign everyone was intently listening and agreed with the changes.

Fast forward two months, all my changes seemed to be backfiring on me. Employees seemed confused and disengaged. The system implementation was not on track. The CEO was starting to hear through the grapevine that I wasn't a good boss. Something about me forcing changes on the team abruptly. Something about me not explaining the why behind my changes. "But I know what I'm doing and they should trust me," I thought. **My employees didn't need to know.**

~

TOO MUCH, TOO FAST

"What do they mean their employees didn't need to know? Of course they do," you might be thinking.

There are two things at play here—a leader who came on too strong, too fast, and employees who saw changes coming their way, too many, too fast. All of it came together in a chaotic mess that resulted in none of it coming together for the good of the business.

While the new Director of Operations had the experience, the drive, and the right idea, sometimes that's not enough. Their approach was misinterpreted and it resulted in a failed adoption of the changes they set out to make. *Hasta las mejores intenciones pueden ser malinterpretadas.*

BRINGING ON A NEW LEADER

As your business transforms, you'll reach a point where you need to hire leaders to help you lead your business. It's no longer feasible to lead everything on your own, and you want to bring in expertise to help you move the business forward. However, you want to be careful with how they're brought in and work with them as to what that transition looks like.

Any new leader should take time to evaluate the existing landscape when they come on board. They should understand existing processes and systems, and why they existed in the first place. They should take the time to get to know the employees because there could be dynamics that need to be uncovered first. It would serve them well to sit back and observe first. Only then will they be in the best position to execute on their vision in a way that impacts your business positively.

EMPLOYEE TRUST AND INSIGHTS

The other benefit of onboarding thoughtfully is that the new leader not only learns the landscape and meets everyone, but they also get a chance to build a better relationship with your employees.

It helps them gain employees' trust, which can be invaluable when implementing changes on a large scale. Your employees will be less likely to question everything they do because they've gotten to know them. And employees are more likely to adopt what they decide to implement, instead of being dismissive of or disengaged from the changes. It also helps them gain insights into your employees' appetite for change, which will help them determine how fast or slow to implement changes.

Particularly if you've been operating with a small, close-knit team of family and friends as some of our businesses have, there'll be a natural resistance to let others in and adopt changes they want to make. You'll want to ensure they take the right approach and also assist them in getting integrated into the team. *Tendrás mejor éxito.*

THE WHY BEHIND THE CHANGES

Change is hard. When a new leader comes in and changes the way of doing things, it can cause friction, especially when employees are used to a certain way of doing things, and a certain leader doing things. And while some friction is natural, too much, and all at once, can be a disaster because you risk the new leader never fully integrating. You risk employees being confused and spending more time talking about them, or complaining about the changes, than doing the work that needs to be done in your business. It shifts the focus away from high-impact work, which is what we're here to do!

Whenever you know you'll have many changes, take the time to explain the rationale behind the changes. *El porqué.*

Employees seek transparency because they want to understand why changes are happening, and how long they have to adjust to changes. They want to feel part of the process, not told or "voluntold" what to do. The more employees understand why you're doing what you're doing, the more they're keen on helping to implement it. Bring employees along for the ride as much as possible. This can start from the moment you decide to bring on someone new. (And even if they don't like the change, involving them and walking through the why will help them wrap their heads around it much easier.)

A CHANGE LAB CAN HELP

I know we don't want more meetings, but this is a different kind of meeting.

A **change lab** is a two-to-three-hour meeting where employees, leaders, and stakeholders come together to discuss a specific change. During this meeting, you work through all the elements, responsibilities, potential issues, and future actions that are involved to bring it to life. You have the chance to explain to them what you want to do. You're able to get their perspective on how they feel about it. You get to openly discuss what could go wrong, and how you can prevent it. It's a great way to manage change. It can be facilitated by you, a designated project sponsor, or a consultant.

It's also a great opportunity to communicate that while you do have ideas, you don't know exactly how everything will turn out and likely some things won't go as planned. You'll need their patience, openness, and empathy as these changes take place. In return, you can offer them a safe space to express their opinions, without them being taken personally (and don't take them personally).

Change management risk is something you want to address proactively, and a change lab is a great way to do it.

THINK ABOUT YOUR BIG CHANGES

Become friends with this risk by walking into a big change with the understanding of your current state, adequate planning for and consideration of the changes being made, and well-thought-out messaging for your employees. What's the next big change you're going to make in your business, and how will you ensure its success and adoption by your employees? Are there any leaders you're planning to hire, and how will you ensure they transition into the business well? Are there any changes where a change lab will help?

We hired fast and it backfired.
POV: CEO and Founder

To witness our growth the last three years was incredible.

Customers couldn't get enough. They loved us. They bought from us and raved about us to their friends.

Along with our sales growth came team growth. The first few years we grew our team super intentionally, adding on key hires when it was the right time and as we had the capacity to onboard. We built a small but mighty team of about thirty employees that loved working for us.

The following year, our growth skyrocketed even more. Each team requested more full-time heads. It felt appropriate given our growth because more sales equal more people needed, right? Where we once had thoughtful intention, we now had swift action. We told people to hire who they needed. We updated our practices to more of a hands-off approach. Before we knew it, we grew our business to fifty, to seventy, and soon we had reached a huge milestone—one hundred employees. We celebrated with a party.

Then slowly, it came crashing down.

Our sales started slipping. Considering our hyper growth initially, we thought it was just leveling out. But it didn't stop, and soon the graph was trending downward. The tide that had brought us thousands of customers was now turning. Not because they didn't like our product, but because they were choosing to spend money in other ways, on other things. It also didn't help us that the economy tanked during this time. Our forecasts were consistently off. When it came time to plan the next year, we presented a loss of millions and our investors laughed. "Come up with a better plan," they said. "You're going to have to do layoffs," they said. We hadn't done layoffs before, but we knew it was the easiest way to cut costs.

Our first layoff was painful. Trust was broken with our employees.

It didn't stop us from having hope. We had a plan, and even told our remaining employees it would not happen again. Ironically, a few months later, we did another layoff…and a few small secret rounds that we hoped no one noticed. **We hired fast and it backfired.**

~

SOMETIMES WE GET EXCITED

It's easy to get excited when you see hyper growth in your business. You see sales rolling in. You see more cash in your bank accounts. You hire one, five, ten people to support the growth. You start to transform your business into what you think will serve you long term. But if you aren't careful, before you know it, you're transforming too fast.

Unfortunately, in this story, the CEO did just that. Their business seemed to be going to infinity and beyond, so they got overly excited. They started moving five steps at a time, instead of moving one step at a time. They hired at a rapid speed without stopping to think about each move they were making. It was inevitable that it would catch up to them. *Era sólo cuestión de tiempo.*

THE RIPPLE EFFECT OF LAYING PEOPLE OFF

Layoffs have consequences. There's more to it than just the immediate relief of reducing your expenses. You risk changing the course of your business if your operations can't adjust to the transition. You risk losing trust from your employees, something which is hard to recover. Plus, you risk your public perception being affected if your layoffs make headlines.

And to the person on the receiving end of a layoff, they're left surprised, confused, frustrated, and all the emotions in between. They trusted a company and their values. They relied on their salary to support their family, buy a home, or pay loans off. Especially for many of us who're trying to build wealth for ourselves and our communities, it's a shock to the system. *Un shock total.* (Layoffs are personal no matter what some might say.)

WHO'S TO BLAME

It might be tempting to blame the economy or chalk it up to business as usual, but layoffs signal something deeper is going on. *Hay más bajo la superficie.*

Let's bring back the root cause analysis tool we learned earlier in this book, where we ask why, and why again, a few times, to get a better idea of what really caused these layoffs. Because only then can we prevent it from happening again, and prevent it from happening at all in your business.

So, why did layoffs happen?

- In the first why, it's because the company needed to cut expenses.
- Asking why again, they needed to cut expenses because sales dropped.
- Asking why again, sales dropped because they didn't properly understand their growth (they relied on circumstantial growth instead of identifying real, stable growth).
- Asking why again, they didn't properly understand their growth because they didn't perform adequate strategic planning.

In other words, this could have been prevented with adequate strategic planning around revenue and team growth. It's clear a risk lens was missing throughout their journey.

A risk lens up-front would have allowed them to better assess their business decisions. This would have prompted them to understand more about their revenue growth, which would have influenced their hiring plans. Instead of going into "hire, hire, hire" mode, there would have been a more intentional approach. They might have hired slower.

Or they might have considered hiring part-time employees, temporary employees, or contractors first; these are scenarios where expectations tend to be better aligned. Any of these actions would have put them in the best position to prevent layoffs from happening. *Es prevenible.*

THERE ARE OTHER OPTIONS

Remember that having a risk lens isn't foolproof. It'll put you in the best position, but it doesn't mean everything will go as planned. Things will happen.

If you do find yourself in a position where you need to cut costs, before you go the traditional way businesses do it, explore other ways. We're here to do things differently and take action in innovative ways after all. Are there other expenses you can reduce? Can you leverage the employees in another department based on their skill set? Can you train them with a new skill set? Can you offer them a transition period? Can you refer them to another business?

And if all else fails and there's really no other option, show compassion and empathy when delivering the news.

REFLECT ON YOUR HIRING APPROACH

Think about your approach to team growth for the next year, or few years. What does your hiring strategy look like as you transform? Have you pressure tested it to make sure it's in line with what your business needs, and can handle? Are there signals you might be missing or misinterpreting? Are you putting yourself in the best position to never have to lay off anyone?

Employees are leaving in droves—was it me?
POV: CEO and Founder

When I first started out, I had huge aspirations for my business.

I wrote out the values I swore we would live by. It would be all about the people. It would be all about integrity. It would be about work-life balance. And I did just that. I was very intentional about the values and culture that I wanted to create. Everything from the hiring experience and employee experience to employee communications was carefully crafted so that everyone felt like they belonged. I welcomed every new hire personally. We had it all—the town halls, the retreats, the happy hours, the birthday cards. The team camaraderie was top-notch. No one left for the first few years. We had one of the best cultures out there.

It was imperceptible at first, but the culture started to shift as we continued to grow. We formed new departments where each leader led with their own unique style. We started to decentralize how we did things to avoid bottlenecks. Whereas I used to be in every meeting and part of every decision, I was now focused on being the face of the company and wasn't really involved in the day-to-day. My Executive Assistant now sent the welcome emails. I admittedly lost touch with who was joining. And I definitely wasn't notified if people left.

One day, I asked my Executive Assistant to schedule a meeting with our Product Manager who I had spoken to about a project we could do, and they told me they had left. "Oh," I thought, "That's weird. They never reached out." A couple weeks later, I asked about another employee and got the same response. The next day, my VP of Supply Chain put in their notice. "Hmm, when did people start leaving?" I thought. I asked my Executive Assistant how many people had left recently.

*They weren't sure, but said they would ask people operations for a report of employees who had left in the past year. I was shocked when I received the results. **Employees were leaving in droves—was it me?***

~

SOME TURNOVER IS NORMAL

It's completely normal to have some employee turnover in your business. The employee who decides to return to school, go into politics, be a full-time parent, take a sabbatical, or land an amazing role somewhere else—it's all normal. People have different aspirations, chapters, and events in their life that may lead them to pursue other ventures outside of your business. These employees should be celebrated and thanked for their contributions. *No seas ingrata.*

It's less about whether the employee turnover is happening or not, because it likely is, but more about the reasons why. Why are they leaving? How many people are leaving? How fast are they leaving? The risk here isn't that people leave, but whether or not them leaving is signaling that something negative is happening in your business.

IT'S NOT ME, IT'S YOU

Especially as you transform your business with new people, new leaders, new products/markets, and more complex processes, there'll be organizational and cultural shifts that may trigger people to leave.

For one reason or another, they no longer feel aligned with your business. Maybe there are too many changes happening at once, and they feel overwhelmed. Maybe they don't understand some of the changes, and they feel disconnected from the vision. Maybe they're used to working on one team and since the business has split into multiple teams, they don't feel supported in their immediate team (microcultures can develop as you separate teams). Or it could also be that they aren't happy with new leadership because they operate under other beliefs and norms that are different from your business. It could originate as far back as when they were hired and the expectations didn't match the reality they found themselves in, in terms of their responsibilities or their work hours, for instance.

Whatever the reason, you won't be able to identify it and get ahead of it in your business unless you're actively applying a risk lens. In this story, the turnover was happening for a while, but it wasn't brought front and center until it happened to stand out to the CEO. Employees had started to leave at increasing rates, but no one was monitoring it or reporting out on it.

Employees keep your business running. *Préstales atención, por favor.*

PAY ATTENTION TO EMPLOYEE TURNOVER

If you're in this scenario, a good risk response would be to conduct an **employee turnover analysis** because you don't want something bigger going on here than just a few employees leaving. You want to better understand why you're unable to retain your talent.

To conduct it, you'd first pull a report of employees that recently left and calculate your employee turnover rate. Then you'd go through the list of employees and separate out the employees you aren't worried about, the ones that left for "normal" reasons (not a signal that something's wrong). For those remaining, you'd identify the reasons why they left via exit surveys or interviews, and seek out any trends. Are there leaders who have employees leaving under them more than others? Are there employees who felt like the hiring process was misleading? Are there employees who feel like things have changed in your business?

Based on your findings, you'd take action. This could involve talking to those leaders who have too many people under them leaving, improving the hiring process if expectations are unclear during the interviews, or spending more time communicating changes so employees don't feel out of the loop.

RED FLAG ALERT

A quick callout to a big red flag.

When someone leaves within a year, it's a huge signal to you that something isn't working. You spent hours interviewing them, training them, welcoming them, only for them to leave within a year, and have to do it all over again. It's a huge waste of resources that you and the hiring team could have dedicated to bigger and better things. Even if just a few employees left this year, it all adds up. (When this happens, it should prompt you to dedicate attention to it because you want to prevent this in the future. Consider speaking to the employee directly before they leave too.)

LET'S APPLY IT TO YOUR BUSINESS

Determine your employee turnover rate for the last year.

If it's high, or higher than you expected, go ahead and perform an employee turnover analysis for your business using the guidance from above, and take action based on the results. And for future years, consider setting up a threshold for what turnover rate will trigger a detailed analysis.

If it's zero or low, move on to other risks. Your ability to retain talent doesn't need to be high on your radar. *Lo puedes ignorar por ahora.* (And that's okay because our risks evolve with us as we transform. It might not be a risk now, but now you know to pay attention to it once you start hiring and managing bigger teams).

Chapter 12

Keep Your Business Aligned with Its Purpose: Meaning Well and Doing Well Can Become Two Different Things If You Don't Transform Thoughtfully

Y ou started your business to impact in a big way. Whether it's a commitment to amplifying diversity, protecting the environment, elevating your communities, or all three, you want your business to impact beyond what it sells. And while your intentions might be well-meaning, if you don't see your impact initiatives through to authentic execution, they can fall short and even be detrimental to your reputation. In this chapter, we'll walk through how you can stay aligned with your purpose as you transform, and then we'll close out this final chapter by talking about how being aware of your risk ecosystem will protect you, your business, and your impact.

Did they actually care, or was it performative?
POV: DEI Program Lead

The decision came from the top—it was time to implement a diversity, equity, and inclusion (DEI) program.

Our customers wanted it, our employees wanted it, and our board wanted it. We always believed in giving our stakeholders what they wanted.

I thought this was the beginning of something wonderful for the business. We got a budget approved and identified a program sponsor. Next, we needed a program manager to lead us in this endeavor. I was tapped for it and told I would transition out of my current role. It didn't feel like I had much of a choice, if I'm being honest. I was a damn good Head of Product, but I guess I was the perfect face to be the new DEI Program Lead as an Afro-Latina.

We built out a program framework and outlined the commitments that we aimed to achieve over the next three years. We also assembled a team of employees who would do stretch assignments with the program as we got it off the ground.

We proceeded to publicly announce our commitments to show that we were taking this seriously. It was of course well received in the media and by our employees. We started making progress and integrating DEI into our marketing, hiring, sourcing, and community efforts—doing extended focus groups alongside marketing campaigns, reviewing our hiring practices, training employees on the importance of diversity and how to recognize unconscious bias, sourcing diverse suppliers, and donating money—among many other things. It felt like we were making progress, and we were.

At least early on we were.

But eventually, it seemed like progress stalled. We could feel the resistance. It didn't seem like everyone was on board anymore. At our program check-ins, the team still kept telling us they were making progress, but it seemed like the details seemed to get more and more vague. The public no longer got regular updates. I brought it up to our program sponsor and leadership, but I was told we had other more pressing issues.

Week after week, month after month. Same thing.

About a year into the program, a bad economy meant budget cuts—and guess what was the first to go? Our DEI program. "We no longer have the funds," they said. "We could revisit at a later time," they said. Even though they said they saw the social impact and the economic benefits, did they? I had no choice but to leave.

Shortly after, there was an article published about them. The headline read: **Did they actually care, or was it performative?**

~

THE SYSTEM DOESN'T VALUE DEI

The reports, data, case studies—they all show DEI has a positive business impact. But why is it so hard for businesses to get on board? Why do businesses still see it as a cost? Why do they pretend to care when they don't?

Frankly, it's the system. *No nos sorprende.*

The problem is the system still packages it as a nice-to-have versus a need-to-have. While our communities understand the importance of diverse backgrounds, perspectives and experiences, equitable opportunities, and the safety in inclusive spaces, the rest of society and most businesses have yet to catch up.

DEI is still seen as a separate department or set of responsibilities that take away from other priorities. ("Why should we hire two DEI heads instead of hiring two business development heads?") We're still in a system that sees it as a cost and not as something that should be embedded for the good of the business. This is why when it comes time to cut expenses, it's the first to go. Plus, many unfortunately see DEI programs as an opportunity to pretend they care to garner the public's affection, when in reality they don't value it.

COMMIT OR DON'T, THERE'S NO IN BETWEEN

The sad part is the risk goes even further than whether or not a business is overlooking a DEI program for creating positive business impact. By making promises and then breaking them, businesses risk their reputation in the eyes of their employees, customers, and the public.

Anytime you commit to something and go back on it, it signals to your employees and the street where your priorities lie, and that you aren't true to your word.

Performatism is running rampant these days, meaning businesses are saying one thing, but continuing to make the same harmful choices and actions. So many businesses are showcasing their DEI programs, initiatives, and commitments because they think it's expected, without being fully invested. *Por favor*, people see through this.

Your employees sure do. I guarantee it. Every time they hear, "We care about our people. We're all about listening and creating a safe space," they roll their eyes. *Te lo prometo.* They see it when your commitment is to have a diverse set of candidates for roles, but you already had someone slated for the role before anyone else had a chance to apply. They see it when top leaders don't take the unconscious bias or inclusive environment trainings seriously, or even take them at all.

Employees see through performative DEI, and it feels like a slap in the face. *Una cachetada que arde.* Because once you see it, it's hard to unsee. And this is where you risk employees becoming disengaged, calling out sick, taking leaves, or quiet quitting. The whispers become abundant. This affects morale, productivity, and ultimately, your bottom line. You risk tanking your reputation with your employees if you play pretend.

Consumers are also becoming way more aware of who they're buying from. They pay attention to who speaks up against social issues and injustices. They pay attention to who stays quiet and hopes it passes. They actually want you to proudly stand behind what you believe in so they can make informed decisions about where to shop.

The last thing they want is to shop from a business that's catering to popular opinion and paying lip service.

LESS TOKENISM, MORE RECOGNITION

And please, don't force others to take on diverse roles just because they're diverse and would be a good token or figurehead for the program. If they're good at their job, leave them there. Otherwise, it defeats the purpose. We don't want all diverse individuals to be picked out and placed onto a DEI team. We can do other things... *¿Cierto, o cierto?*

In that same vein, DEI work doesn't just magically happen either. It's one of the most common forms of unpaid labor—yes, many love it and have a passion for it, but it's work. Anyone who's leading employee resource groups (ERGs), taking stretch assignments in DEI initiatives, or conducting trainings in addition to their job should be appropriately recognized for their efforts. It could be compensated for in the form of a bonus or additional vacation days. At the very least, it should be part of their performance plan. It's not a case of, "Well you asked for it. Now you do it all."

EMBED IT FOR TRUE IMPACT

Believe it or not, it's not about building a huge DEI team. Yes, you may have to bring on a team to execute the transformation, but if the job is done right, DEI is so far embedded into how each department operates, how the strategy is built, how products are created, how campaigns are carried out, and how employee experiences are curated. The need for a large DEI team disappears when it's embedded. You're left with one or two heads to help you project manage and monitor specific initiatives or commitments.

FIVE PILLARS TO A GREAT DEI APPROACH

I don't doubt that DEI is important to you, but don't sleep on the performative aspect. You have to walk the talk and validate that what you committed to doing you did.

A proper DEI approach will set you up for success. At its core, it should center on a few primary pillars, a few KPIs that'll measure how well you're doing, and an accountability mechanism that'll ensure it's taken seriously.

Consider the following **five DEI pillars** as a great starting point. Remember that it goes beyond just your employees. It's about how your business *as a whole* approaches DEI.

- **Product** – How are products developed? Does R&D think about a diverse customer base as they develop their product assortment, features or functionalities?

- **Customers** – Does marketing have inclusive practices? Are you speaking to all your customers, or do most of your campaigns speak to a select demographic?

- **Suppliers** – Who are your main suppliers? Do you seek out suppliers that are women owned? Do you seek out suppliers of color? Do you attend supplier conferences that specialize in diversity?

- **Employees** – What are your employee demographics? Is it representative of the population? Are your hiring practices equitable?

- **Community** – What organizations, clubs, or charities are you working with? Are you serving diverse communities?

Next, determine the KPIs you want to track. Because if it doesn't get measured, it doesn't get managed. This could be what percentage of diverse businesses you work with (e.g., women or minority owned, small businesses), what percentage of employees are women/men/ nonbinary in leadership roles, and, by ethnicity, what percentage of roles have a diverse candidate within the interview slate—or what percentage of marketing campaigns include input from various perspectives before launching. There are endless ones you can choose from and you should curate the ones that work for your business.

As for your accountability mechanism, put someone in charge to oversee your DEI approach, whether it's you, another employee, or a specific DEI program lead. But the keyword here is "oversee"— because you want to make sure it's not just the DEI program lead who's accountable for execution. Everyone on your team has to know what part they play, and it should be tied to their performance plan in some way.

And finally, if you're planning to put out public DEI commitments, make sure you really can stand behind them and authentically believe in them. Otherwise, everyone will see right through it, and if that happens, you risk being a front-page headline or a viral video, tanking your reputation along with it!

WHAT'S YOUR DEI APPROACH?

Write out your DEI approach using the five pillars above. As everything else, it'll transform over time, becoming more complex as your business moves through each stage. Be sure to check in with it regularly to ensure the approach still works with your business. Stand behind it and stay committed to it so you can live out your business ethos with pride.

Our social and sustainability claims were questionable.

POV: Senior Manager of Impact

I always wanted to work for a purpose-driven business, and it finally happened.

I was hired as Senior Manager of Impact for a business that was on a mission to drive change through sustainable products for everyday living. They cared about the planet and its people. They spent extensive time researching and sourcing recyclable materials and packaging. They aimed to achieve gender and pay equity amongst their employees. They had plans to diversify their supplier base too. My job was to help them bring all their impact initiatives under one umbrella, with an ultimate goal to create and distribute an Impact Report to share with the public.

Once I had learned enough about each initiative, I developed an outline for our Impact Report. I assigned each statistic, data point, or blurb to the relevant team member, and requested they provide the required information. It took a bit of chasing and following up, but I got everything we needed together. I compiled it and started working with a graphic designer to make sure the report was on-brand. Several drafts later, it was ready to be reviewed by our leadership team with final approval by our CEO.

One last thing I wanted to do was bring in an outside set of eyes to review our Impact Report because I knew how important it was for our reputation, and I wanted to get it right. We thought it would be a quick check to give us final comfort.

Oh, were we wrong.

The consultant came in and validated our Impact Report against source information, and their findings report revealed that some of the claims could open us up for liability. For instance, we claimed all our products were recyclable, but not all our packaging was so it could be perceived as misleading. Our statistics also weren't always correct, either because the data wasn't accurate, or was across the wrong time period, and some didn't even have backup information. Plus, to top it off, the report was supposed to cover a specific year, but our gender and pay equity data was from two years prior. We were all over the place.

The consultant strongly recommended that we reconsider publishing the report to the public until we could correct or live up to the representations we were making. ***Our social and sustainability claims were questionable.***

~

YOU MAKE REPRESENTATIONS WITH OR WITHOUT A REPORT

Do you currently have an impact report? Maybe, maybe not.

But you started your business to make an impact, so in one form or another, you're likely making representations, or claims, about that impact. It might be on your website. It might be in your marketing materials. It might be on your product labels. It might be anytime you speak at an event—at a conference, networking party, investors' luncheon, vendor market, expo, etc.

For example, you might claim that your business is:

- Manufacturing products with nontoxic ingredients.
- Sourcing packaging materials that are eco-friendly.
- Making decisions that lower your carbon footprint.
- Upcycling and repurposing discarded goods.
- Worrying about your end-to-end supply chain ethics.
- Diversifying your suppliers to empower small businesses.
- Hiring locally to support your community.
- Paying fairly and equitably, regardless of gender, race, ethnicity or other status.
- Donating to charity or supporting specific social causes.

Anytime you make any of these claims, you want to make sure that you can back it up with cold, hard facts, not lukewarm facts that may be kinda, sorta true. Otherwise, you'll risk ending up in a vulnerable position as they did in this story. Thankfully they had the right idea to hire a consultant to help validate their claims before the report went public, but not everyone will be so lucky.

CONSUMERS ARE WAKING UP

More than ever, consumers are seeking out products and services that are environmentally friendly and socially conscious. These can often be the deciding factors for choosing a specific product, or going with a specific service. Consumers want to spend their money on businesses that are driven by impact, and are aligned with their values.

And most are willing to pay a premium to know that their goods are made with ethically sourced fabrics, their food is organic or harvested locally, or the business they're shopping from is committed to investing in the community.

The great news is that since you started your business to make an impact, you already have a superpower to use here. You already aim to build something beyond yourself that changes the way we do things. You already recognize that it's possible to build a business that prioritizes both purpose and profit. It's not without its own challenges, but we aren't strangers to challenges. *Vamos a darle con todo.*

IT'S INGRAINED IN US

Not to mention that for many of us, we also have another superpower ingrained in us because it's already in our culture to be eco-friendly and socially responsible, whether or not we recognized it growing up.

The way we stored containers to reuse later for something completely unrelated, the way we collected bags upon bags to repurpose as trash bags instead of buying actual trash bags, the way we saved gift wrapping to wrap another gift, the way we cleaned with old socks to give them one last use before discarding them, the way we made clothes last for as long as possible by mending them, or the way some of us took suitcases of clothes back to family when we visited them. (Ask me about the clothes I wore in high school that now my sixteen-year-old cousin is happy to wear as "vintage" clothing.)

We've provided massive amounts of items a second, third, fourth life, and we should be proud of that. *Muy orgullosas.*

ALWAYS VERIFY WHAT YOU'RE CLAIMING

We all get excited and dream big and share what we want to achieve, but we want to make sure we can stand behind the claims we're making. The risk here is that while trying to build a business that values impact, you expose yourself to liabilities that could put your business's reputation on the line.

In other words, it's not just the way you design your impact strategy, but also in how you carry it out that's important. You want to become friends with risk by not just understanding how your business approaches impact, but understanding how you'll present and validate the claims, statistics, and metrics that you share.

Because the last thing that you want is to make statements that are proved to be inaccurate or, worse, completely fabricated. *¿Qué va a decir la gente?*

THE ULTIMATE INSULT

Specifically when dealing with the statements we make with regards to the environment, there's a common term, or insult, that you may have seen out there: greenwashing. It was originally coined by environmentalist Jay Westerveld as a way to indicate that a business is falsely promoting how eco-friendly they are, by downplaying other non-eco-friendly actions.

In essence, it means you're telling half truths to get consumers to buy in. It means that you're misleading consumers into thinking that your product or service is doing more to protect the environment that it really is. I don't want anyone to ever use those words in relation to your business!

A beautiful business has to be beautiful inside and out. You won't go far without holding yourself accountable to the truth. *Sin vivir de apariencias, por favor.*

YOU MAY HAVE HEARD OF ESG

Antes de que te me pierdas. ESG is just a fancy acronym, but it's relevant to all businesses regardless of size.

ESG stands for environmental, social, and governance and it's an overarching set of standards that has emerged in recent years and become increasingly popular among the public and investors. As an evolved version of corporate social responsibility (CSR), it broadens how we should build our businesses so that we can both have financial success *and* serve a greater good. It's all about how you pay attention to the environment, how you think about social causes, and how you govern (your business) ethically.

Sin complicarnos, it's the impact your business has. And I bring it up because I want you to be prepared since it's likely you'll be seeing more and more of this term as you grow and scale your business.

APPLY THE SÍARM FRAMEWORK TO
YOUR IMPACT STRATEGY

Remember that we started our business to make an impact, but what type of impact we make is up to us. When developing your impact strategy, consider what's most important to you and your business.

Let's call on the SÍARM framework to help us one last time as we near the end of this book (I know, it went by too fast!).

- **Strategize** – Develop your impact strategy. What do you want your business to stand for and why? What will success be based on? What claims, statistics, or metrics do you plan to measure? And how will you report out on your impact? Will it be with your team, with investors and/or with an impact report?

- **Identify** – Identify your risks. What are the top risks that'll prevent your business from delivering on its impact strategy? What will impede you from getting where you envision going? What could go wrong in how you gather and present results?

- **Assess** – Assess your risks. Do you have enough in place to mitigate the risks you've identified, so that what could go wrong doesn't go wrong? Is everything already in place, or is there something missing? Do you know who's responsible for helping you manage each risk? This is the part where you ensure you have built-in accountability mechanisms so that all claims, statistics, and metrics are correct. If you don't, proceed to "Respond" in the next step of this framework.

- **Respond** – Respond based on your assessment. To execute an effective impact strategy and present your results accurately, what do you need to do? Do you need to strengthen your process? Do you need more resources? Do you need to reprioritize your time? Do you need to hire someone to help you validate everything? Take the actions you need to in order to manage your risks to an acceptable level that works for you and your risk appetite.

- **Monitor** – Monitor your impact strategy. How often will you review it and verify that everything is working as intended?

Following the SÍARM framework will keep you impacting now and for the long term. I can't wait to see how you showcase your impact!

I thought my lawyer was all I needed.
POV: CEO and Founder

My lawyer was with me pretty much from the beginning.

First as a contractor, then on retainer, and eventually they came on full-time to build the next chapter with us.

We trusted them and relied on them to protect us. They were such an asset to us. They helped us with it all — customers, suppliers, vendors, employees, contractors. They drafted contracts. They negotiated contracts. They pointed out potential liabilities. They alerted us to red flags. They looked out for our risks.

Though now looking back on it, it was too much.

One day, we had a board meeting and the board asked us about how we managed risk. "Our lawyer does," we answered. "They're so on top of it," we continued. We went on and on about how much they helped us. The board member who asked the question stopped us and said, "But what about your finances? How do you know your numbers are accurate?" "And what about your policies? How do you know employees follow them?" "And your employees, do they know the role they play?" I had no answer prepared for all their questions because I assumed my lawyer managed all risks for us. I told them I would get back to them.

I went straight to my lawyer after and told them what happened.

*They smiled and said, "Yes, I look out for your legal risks, but there are plenty of other risks you should have a handle on as well. I've actually been meaning to bring this up to you because I feel a big responsibility to protect your business and it's quite overwhelming." I was caught off guard. **I thought my lawyer was all I needed.***

~

YOUR LAWYER CAN'T DO IT ALL

Having a great lawyer is fantastic. Give them their flowers. *Se lo merecen*. But you can't rely on them for managing all your risks.

First, because as we know, we all manage risk—you, your team, everyone, at every level, so relying on them to manage all your risks is unfair to them and your business. Second, because your lawyer doesn't know everything about every situation, it would be irresponsible for them to provide an opinion without context or limited information. A lawyer's favorite answer is, "It depends," and that's for good reason. They don't have eyes everywhere.

Thinking narrowly about risks could lead you to having tunnel vision and missing other risks that are important as they did in this story. You want your business to be well supported by a risk ecosystem that'll protect you as you transform.

ALWAYS PAY ATTENTION TO LEGAL RISK

Before I go into your risk ecosystem and how it evolves, let's address legal risk because it's no doubt one of the top risks you should be paying attention to as you build your beautiful business. And unfortunately, it's the one that can fall to the bottom of the to-do list if you get caught up getting things to market and making sales.

Two key legal items to consider are contracts and intellectual property, also known as IP. (Not to be confused with indirect procurement, which also has the acronym of IP.)

- **Contracts** – It can't be overstated that contracts will protect you. They will make expectations clear on both sides and they're an easy go-to to resolve any confusion, especially in the case of disputes. This goes for customers, vendors, and employees. A customer contract could confirm pricing terms, chargeback criteria, and your refund policy. A vendor contract could outline payment terms, quality expectations, and a code of conduct. An employee contract could determine salary, bonus, and type of employment (at-will, contractor, etc.).

- **Intellectual Property** – Always protect your intellectual property (IP) because there are plenty of bad actors out there who will take their chance to copy what you have developed. Intellectual property includes things like patents, copyrights, trademarks, and trade secrets. If you have a patent on a specific product because of its shape, design, technology, don't sleep on starting the patent process. And if you know you have a specific name, logo, slogan, whether it's for your business or a specific product or program you have, start the trademark process early because it can take over a year to go through.

Whichever stage you're in, you'll want to find out which approach to mitigating legal risk is right for your business. Likely, similar to this story, you'll want a lawyer who can be on-call when you're emerging, on retainer as you're growing, and in-house once you're scaling. It's a cost that's well worth it. Find yourself a great lawyer!

Plus, the great news is that the legal landscape is changing. It used to be the case that lawyers were only out to nickel-and-dime you, but now there are many lawyers out there who're dedicated to serving their communities with affordable quality legal services. This could look like a fixed price for a contract templates package or trademarking services, or a subscription model for monthly legal services that includes resources and personalized contract reviews.

But always remember, they can't be everything to you. If you're working with them as a contractor or on retainer, make sure you're conscious and cautious about over relying on them, because they aren't with you day-to-day, so they don't know everything about your business.

INTRODUCING THE THREE LINES MODEL

Okay, back to your risk ecosystem. There's a useful framework created by The Institute of Internal Auditors called the **Three Lines Model** that delegates risk responsibilities across your business. Stay with me. *No te me pierdas.* It's not that bad.

It essentially exists to help us understand what part each of us plays and how we can best protect our businesses. Not surprisingly, it consists of three lines.

The first line consists of the employees, or contractors, who provide the product or service that you sell, as well as those who provide support to make it happen. Those who fall within the "direct bucket" are sourcing, inventory, product, sales, wholesale, R&D, customer service, etc. Those who fall into the "support bucket" include finance, accounting, tax, IT, etc. Your first line is present as soon as you start a business. The first line manages risk and the earlier they know that, the better off you'll be.

The second line consists of the employees, or contractors, who provide assistance with managing risk. They help you set standards, develop frameworks, keep you compliant, and report out on how well your business is managing risk. You go to them for guidance, expertise, and oversight.

Likely the first person you'll have on your second line is your lawyer, and rightfully so. And then as you grow your business, you'll evolve into also having other compliance and risk management focused team members. This could include compliance with product regulations, quality assurance, cybersecurity, internal controls, and enterprise risk management. Depending on your business, you might hire some of these sooner than later, and others you may never hire at all.

The third line consists of the employees, or contractors, who provide an independent view of it all. This is typically known as internal audit. They help you validate that your risks are being managed. As their name indicates, they're internal, but they're also independent, which means that while they want you to achieve your goals, they're objective when assessing your business and bringing to light any significant issues. They're your strategic partner, trusted advisor, and value driver that ensures your business doesn't just think its operating a certain way, but validates that it is.

YOUR RISK ECOSYSTEM WILL EVOLVE

The Three Lines Model is operating in your business whether you know it or not so you might as well pay attention to it. It's critical to keeping your business beautiful long-term.

In your early days when you wear all the hats, the lines are likely blurred, with the exception of your lawyer who's there to help you with your second line. And that's okay.

But when you start to hire, you should onboard employees and contractors with risk education right off the bat. Talk to them about which line they're assisting you with because it all starts with awareness. They should know what part they play in your business.

As for the second line, I may be a bit biased, but if you're still with me, you understand the importance of becoming friends with risk, so I'll go ahead and say that, in my humble opinion, you should start building it out early on in your business. You're managing risk from day one, so you want to bring on a risk management professional as soon as you have the time and funds to.

And this doesn't mean you have to hire someone full time. You can start with a risk advisor or a risk project. A risk advisor would provide support on an ongoing basis for a few hours every month or quarter—someone you can lean on for that extra set of eyes to help you identify and proactively get ahead of risks. Or you can start with a risk project, a business risk assessment, where you'll get a full report that tells you what your top risks are, specific areas where you're exposed with expert recommendations on how to move forward, and where you're well-protected. Managing risk is about knowing where you're doing well too.

It's well worth the investment because having that peace of mind is invaluable. It comes down to whether or not you would rather invest a few thousand in a risk advisor or a business risk assessment, or lose several thousand because you missed something and it turned out to be a big mistake. As we've seen throughout this book, there are many mistakes that can be made. And the whole point of this book is for you to avoid them!

As for the third line, I would start thinking about it once you're transforming from your growing to your scaling stage. You want to be somewhat established in your business with processes and policies that you can actually audit against. As for how big your internal audit department should be, well, in Fortune 500 companies, the internal audit department can be a twenty-to-thirty-five-person team. *¡No te asustes!* I won't recommend that. Once you're ready, hire a fractional internal audit contractor that does an independent business risk assessment and a couple of audits every year to help you validate how well you're managing risk. And then as you continue to scale, you can hire, or outsource, a full-time internal audit person or team and increase the number of audits you perform annually.

IDENTIFY YOUR NEXT STEPS

Long story short, a lawyer doesn't manage all your risks! Become friends with risk by considering not just legal risk, but also considering your risk ecosystem. This way you'll be able to get ahead and stay ahead of risks. (And you'll be prepared the next time your board, or a potential investor, asks you about risk management.)

So, what are your next steps? Do you need to stop relying on your lawyer for too much? Will you map out your three lines? Are you going to teach your team about the Three Lines Model? Is it time to consider hiring a risk advisor or performing a business risk assessment? How do you see your risk ecosystem evolving over time? Write out your next three steps and actions you'll take, with specific deadlines to hold yourself accountable.

Pasito a pasito, you'll have a great risk ecosystem to support your beautiful business.

Conclusion

A nd you made it to the end of this book — you're now a beautiful business builder! *¡Felicidades!* Together, we've redefined how to think about risk, and discovered how to use it as a powerful enabler for your business.

Now you know exactly why embedding a risk lens in your business from your mindset, strategy, and processes to your transformations will allow you to grow, scale, and make your impact without the stress, overwhelm, and headaches. And you have the risk strategies, frameworks, and tools to build a beautiful business and avoid mistakes that other businesses have made.

You're more than ready to disrupt your way into a better future armed with knowledge that no one can take away from you. Making great decisions, creating the right strategies, sorting big ideas, charting the optimal path, deciding to greenlight or sunset processes, organizing projects well — it's all at your fingertips:

- The SÍARM risk management framework will have you feeling confident with every single decision you make in your business (chapter 2).

- The five-step strategy blueprint will set up your business to thrive year after year (chapter 4).

- The HMMM strategy approach will help you sift through your ideas to decide if a strategy will work for you before you embark on it (chapter 5).

- The integrated analysis will support you in determining whether a process should continue (chapter 8).

- The PPT framework will make sure you don't overlook any important elements as you map out solutions for your business (chapter 10).

- The six-step project plan will prepare every one of your projects for success (chapter 10).

Not to mention that you have tools that are on call to help you, like the root cause analysis, RACI chart, and change lab (chapters 8, 10, and 11), along with examples of risk assessments you can apply to your business like the revenue risk assessment and single-source risk assessment (chapters 2 and 8, respectively) and a ton of examples of internal controls that you can implement (chapters 7 to 10). Plus, more risk terms, risk actions, and risk types, than you've ever asked for, but are now happy you have and can tell your team about so you can curate your risk landscape.

You'll be thinking about risk earlier than most businesses, and putting yourself in the best position to succeed. You'll have fewer odds stacked against you in your journey of building a business and creating impact for our communities. You'll make decisions in your business that'll allow you to build *your* beautiful business *con confianza*.

Plus, risk is now your friend! Remember that what's most important is that you work with risk in a way that works for you in the season that you're in. It's okay for your friendship with risk to evolve, just like real friendships. Sometimes you might be best friends, sometimes you might be learning to get along, and other times you might not like each other much.

I hope you're feeling inspired, supported, and ready to transform how you run your business. I want to help millions of women, BIPOC, and LGBTQIA+ entrepreneurs become the powerhouse leaders and changemakers they were meant to be! I want to empower you and others to see that everything is possible. Because it is, and we can do it. Our contributions are invaluable. I can't wait to see what you do!

So, what's next in your risk journey?

The best part is you can now decide your path. *Tú decides.*

This book might be enough for now. Take what you've learned and implement it in your business. Come back to this book as many times as you need to.

If you want to go beyond this book, head over to the Beautiful Business Center where you'll find value-packed resources, templates, and much more, including a summary of the top risks we discussed in this book, and a quiz that reveals what kind of risk taker you are. This center will be your go-to place for all the latest *chisme* so you can strengthen your friendship with risk over the next few years.

Scan this QR code to enter now,
or visit http://buildabeautifulbusiness.com.

If you want to work together, I invite you to reach out! Whether you're looking for a consulting project, a 1:1 advisor, a workshop, or for me to come speak to your business or organization, please send me a message. I'm here to serve you and maximize the impact we have with our beautiful businesses.

Thank you!
¡Gracias!

Con mucha gratitud,
Rosalie

CAN I ASK YOU A FAVOR?
¿TE PUEDO PEDIR UN FAVOR?

Did you know that only 5 to 10 percent of readers leave book reviews? We're all about changing the statistics here and this is one I'm hoping you can help with.

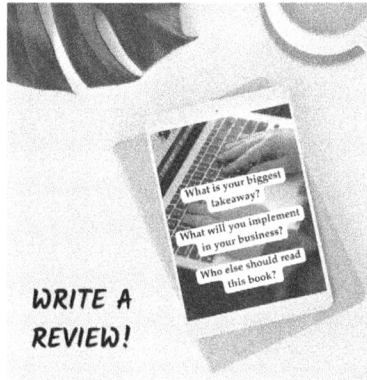

By leaving a review, you'll directly amplify the impact of this book and get it into the hands of someone who needs it. YOUR review may tell a potential reader exactly what they need to know about this book to motivate them to get it!

Whether it's one sentence or a novel, I'd love to hear what you have to say. I read every single review.

Scan this QR code to leave a review now,
or visit http://beautifulbusinessbook.com

Spanish-English Dictionary

Beginning of the Book

A la cultura - To culture
Antes de que nos aplasten como una cucaracha jaja - Before we get squashed like a cockroach haha
Chisme - Gossip
Con confianza - With confidence
¿Empezamos? - Shall we begin?
Escalofríos - Chills
¿Estás lista? - Are you ready?
No te vas a arrepentir. - You won't regret it.
Pero no te me escondas - But don't go and hide
Por si las necesitas en el futuro - In case you need them in the future
¡Qué emoción! - How exciting!
¡Salud! - Cheers!
Se ha dicho - It's been declared
Seguimos adelante como sea. - We keep going no matter what.
Si soy sincera - If I'm honest
¡Te lo prometo! - I promise!
¿Te parece bien? - Sounds good?
¡Todas somos bellas! - We're all beautiful!
¡Unos regalos para ti! - A few gifts for you!

Part 1 - Mindset

Agradéceles. - Thank them.
Centavito(s) - Cent(s) (diminutive)
Claro que sabemos festejar, pero no se pasen. - Of course we know how to have a good time, but don't go overboard.
¿Cómo que no podemos gastar en esto? Siempre lo hemos hecho. - What do you mean we can't spend on this? We've always been able to.
Con confianza - With confidence
Cuanto más fuertes seamos, más impacto tendremos. - The stronger we are, the more impact we'll have.
De donde come uno comen dos. - There's space for everyone. (idiom)
¡Déjalas, por favor! - Leave them alone, please!
Dime con quién andas y te diré quién eres. - Tell me who you surround yourself with and I'll tell you who you are.
¿Estamos listas? - Are we ready?
Evitemos incendios. - Let's avoid fire drills.
Fuera de aquí. - Get out of here.

¿Hablo verdades o no? - It's true, right?
¡Juntas somos más fuertes! - Together we are stronger!
Machista - Sexist
Más o menos - So-so
Más vale prevenir que curar. - Prevention is better than cure.
Me largo de aquí y me voy de vacaciones. - I'm out of here and I'm going on vacation.
Mejor sola que mal acompañada. - You're better off alone than in bad company.
No, gracias. - No, thank you.
No lo pienses tanto. - Don't overthink it.
¡No pare, sigue, sigue! - Don't stop, keep going!
¡Nos estamos poniendo viejitas—jaja! - We're getting old—haha!
Para que no se olviden - So they don't forget
Por favor - Please
Porque somos magníficas - Because we are magnificent
Prepárense. - Get ready.
¿Qué pasa si es un fracaso? - What if it fails?
¡Que te cuenten el chisme! - Let them fill you in!
Repito. - I repeat.
Sí - Yes
Si les da mala espina - If they have a bad feeling about something (idiom)
Sí, por favor. - Yes, please.
¡Sí, se puede! - Yes, you can!
¿Te acuerdas? - Remember those?
Ten cuidado. - Be careful.
Tenemos cosas que hacer y gente para ayudar. - We have things to do and people to help.
Tenemos un problema. - We have a problem.
Todos tienen influencia. - Everyone has influence.
Un pequeño desvío. - A quick detour
Un poquito - A little bit
Vas a llorar. Veremos si de emoción o de tristeza. Probablemente de los dos. - There will be
    tears. We'll see if they're tears of joy or sadness. Probably both.
Y fuera con tonterías - And leave behind any nonsense
Y no les dio vergüenza. - And they weren't ashamed at all.
Ya no hay quien lo quite. - There's no way to remove it.

Part 2 - Strategy

¡Aguas! - Watch out!
Bueno - Okay
Centavitos - Cents (diminutive)
Chisme - Gossip
Como una mala hierba. - Like a weed. (idiom)
Como una telaraña gigante - Like a giant spider web
Date permiso. - Give yourself permission.
¡Echale ganas! - Go for it!
Estarás preparada y lista para lo que sea. - You'll be prepared and ready for anything.

Feliz como una lombriz - Happy as a clam (idiom)
Manos a la obra. - Let's get to work. (idiom)
Mucho dinero - A lot of money
No puedes controlar todo. - You can't control everything.
No queremos eso. - We don't want that.
¡No seas mensa! - Don't be a fool!
Nunca iba a dar resultado. - It was never going to work.
Obviamente - Obviously
Pasemos página. - Let's move on.
Por favor - Please
Preparadita te ves más bonita. - You'll look your best when you're prepared. (A play on a Spanish idiom)
Que no sea en vano. - Don't let it be for nothing.
¿Quién metió la pata? - Who messed up? (idiom)
Quien sea - Whoever
Sería una pesadilla. - It would be a nightmare.
Solo buenas vibras. - Good vibes only.
Somos víctimas de nuestra ambición. - We're victims of our own ambition.
Siempre pasa algo. - Something always comes up.
Terminará en la basura. - It'll end up in the trash.
Una desgracia total. - A total disaster
Y fuera - And you're done
Y los tiburones no perdonan - And the sharks aren't forgiving
Y queremos llegar - And we want to get there

Part 3 - Processes

¡A nadie! - On anyone!
A tu manera y de nadie más. - Your way and no one else's.
Amiga - Friend
Broma, broma. - Just kidding.
Cafecito - Coffee (diminutive)
Centavitos - Cents (diminutive)
Chisme - Gossip
Como se pueda - However we can
¿Cual prefieres? - Which one do you prefer?
Con ojos abiertos - With eyes wide open
Desapareció como un fantasma. - They vanished like a ghost.
El golpe dolerá menos. - It's a softer hit.
¡Evite el dolor de cabeza! - Avoid the headache!
Locura - Madness
Lo hago como me sale. - Let's see how it comes out.
Loro - Parrot
Me parece bien. - Sounds good to me.
Nada que ver. - It's nothing like that.
Nadie quiere estar expuesto. - Nobody wants to be exposed.

¡Necesitamos los centavitos! - We need money coming in!
No les culpes. - Don't blame them.
No me digas? Te digo. - Are you serious? I'm serious.
No queremos que pase otra vez. - We don't want it to happen again.
No te escapas. - You're not off the hook. (idiom)
No te me escondas jaja - Don't go and hide haha
No te pases. - Don't go overboard.
Nos va a hacer llorar la cebolla jaja - The onion is going to make us cry haha
Ojalá que sí. - I hope so.
Pero ojo - But be careful
Por si las moscas - Just in case (idiom)
Porque uno nunca sabe - Because you never know
¡Pues es su culpa! - Well, it's their fault!
¡Qué desgracia! - What a disaster!
Qué vergüenza. - How embarrassing.
Quién manda aquí - Who's in charge
Quieres hacer cosas más interesantes. - You want to do more interesting things.
Se meten por donde sea. - They'll find a way in.
Siempre habrá quienes se aprovechen. Los malagradecidos. - There will always be those
    that take advantage. Those that are ungrateful.
Sin pesadillas - Without nightmares
Somos resilientes. - We are resilient.
Te cuento. - I'll tell you.
Telenovelas - Soap operas
Tienes que protegerte. - You have to protect yourself.
Traición - Betrayal
Uff no, qué horror. - Oof, absolutely horrible.
Un pequeño desvío - A quick detour
Una preciosura - A real beauty
Uyyy no. - No way.
¡Y listo! - And that's it!

Part 4 - Transformation

¿Aceptas esta responsabilidad? - Do you accept this responsibility?
¡Aguántate! - Hold on!
Antes de que te me pierdas - Before I lose you
Centavito - Cent (diminutive)
¿Cierto, o cierto? - Am I right, or am I right?
El porqué - The why
Era sólo cuestión de tiempo. - It was only a matter of time.
Es prevenible. - It's preventable.
Es tu apoyo. - It's your support.
Guau - Wow
Hasta las mejores intenciones pueden ser malinterpretadas. - Even the best intentions can
    be misinterpreted.

Hay más bajo la superficie. - There's more beneath the surface.
Inhala, exhala. - Inhale, exhale.
Lo puedes ignorar por ahora. - You can ignore it for now.
Los números, uff. - Numbers, ugh.
Muy orgullosas - Very proud
No nos sorprende. - Not surprising.
No queremos esto. - We don't want this.
No seas ingrata. - Don't be ungrateful.
¡No te asustes! - Don't get scared!
No te me pierdas. - Stay with me.
¡Nos gusta el chisme! - We enjoy a good story!
Pasito a pasito - Step by step
¡Ponte las pilas! - Be smart about it! (idiom)
Poquito a poquito - Little by little
Por favor - Please
Por un minuto solamente - Just for a minute
Préstales atención, por favor. - Pay attention to them, please.
¿Qué va a decir la gente? - What will people say?
Sabemos esto. - We know this.
Se lo merecen. - They deserve it.
Sería millonaria. - I'd be a millionaire.
¡Sí, se puede! - Yes, you can!
Sin complicarnos - Without complicating things
Sin vivir de apariencias, por favor. - Don't live a life just for show, please. (idiom)
Te lo prometo. - I promise.
Tendrás mejor éxito. - You'll have better success this way.
Un poco complicado - A little complicated
Un shock total - A total shock
Una cachetada que arde - A slap that stings
Una desgracia total. - A total disaster.
Vamos a darle con todo. - We're going to give it our all.
¡Y listo! - And that's it!

End of the Book

Chisme - Gossip
Con confianza - With confidence
Con mucha gratitud - With much gratitude
¡Felicidades! - Congratulations!
¡Gracias! - Thank you!
Tú decides. - You decide.

Note: These translations are subject to interpretation and adjusted to the context in which they're written, so in some instances they may not match the exact translation.

About the Author

ROSALIE ENNES, CPA, CIA, is a risk expert and beautiful business builder. In her thirteen-plus-year career, she's conducted risk assessments, executed audits, led transformations, advised leaders, and educated employees on the importance of risk. By helping businesses effectively manage their top risks across all areas from finance to culture, she's able to create unparalleled value for businesses to protect, optimize, and strengthen themselves for long-term success.

Since starting her career as a Big Four accounting professional, she's had extensive experience working with various types, sizes, and stages of businesses, from public, private, start-ups to small businesses, both domestically and internationally, and across multiple product and service-based industries, including food & beverage, beauty, apparel, and wellness, giving her a unique perspective and integrated approach when it comes to running and leading a business. In 2023, she founded Portecua Consulting to equip impact-driven businesses with a risk lens, with a passion for helping diverse entrepreneurs leverage risk as a powerful way to build their beautiful businesses—because she believes we deserve growth, representation, and wealth just like everyone else. She envisions a future where we're all empowered with the risk mindset, strategies, and tactics to achieve our goals with confidence and peace of mind, and to create intentional impact for our communities.

Rosalie holds dual degrees in Business Administration and Latin American Studies from the University of California, Berkeley. She is a Bay Area native and a proud Ecuadorian-Portuguese American, who enjoys experiencing life through travel, food, and tennis, and with her rescue dog, Kira. She currently resides in New York City.

Website I www.portecuaconsulting.cpa
LinkedIn I www.linkedin.com/in/portecua
Instagram I www.instagram.com/portecuaconsulting
YouTube I www.youtube.com/@portecuaconsulting